90 0872580 0

D1765850

University of Plymouth Library
Subject to status this item may be renewed
via your Voyager account
http://voyager.plymouth.ac.uk
Tel: (01752) 232323

Children as Decision Makers in Education

Also available from Continuum

Thinking Children, Claire Cassidy

Children's Lives, Children's Futures, Paul Croll, Gaynor Attwood & Carol Fuller

Children as Decision Makers in Education

Sharing Experiences Across Cultures

Sue Cox, Caroline Dyer, Anna Robinson-Pant
and Michele Schweisfurth

continuum

Continuum International Publishing Group

The Tower Building
11 York Road
London
SE1 7NX

80 Maiden Lane
Suite 704
New York
NY 10038

www.continuumbooks.com

British Library Cataloguing-in-Publication Data
A catalogue record for this book is available from the British Library.

ISBN: 9780826425485 (hardcover)

Library of Congress Cataloging-in-Publication Data
A catalog record for this book is available from the Library of Congress

Typeset by BookEns, Royston, Herts.
Printed in Great Britain by the MPG Books Group, Bodmin and King's Lynn

Contents

Notes on Contributors

Sheila Aikman is Senior Lecturer in Education and Development at the University of East Anglia. She was formerly the Policy Adviser for Oxfam GB and has been researching and publishing in the areas of quality education, gender equality in education and intercultural education.

Jane Bañez-Ockelford was the Development Director for Asia, South America and the Caribbean for *EveryChild UK* until October 2008 and continues to provide strategic management and technical support to the *EveryChild Cambodia* Liaison Office. Jane currently works within Asia as a consultant in governance and strategic management based in the Philippines.

Juan Carlos Barrón-Pastor (Juancho Barrón) is a PhD candidate and assistant tutor at the School of Development Studies, University of East Anglia, and was recently Visiting Professor at the National Autonomous University of Mexico (UNAM). He has seventeen years of experience in coordinating, administrating, consulting, teaching, and researching for community development projects in Mexico. His current research explores how to interpret the theory of becoming (Deleuze; Braidotti) through an inter-subjectivist approach (Lenkersdorf), taking collective emotions into account (Forgas; Marina) to better understand culturally diverse education spaces.

Teeka Bhattarai has been associated with the School of Ecology, Agriculture and Community Works (Seacow) and Forum for Popular Education – Education Network, in Nepal since their foundation. Currently undertaking formal studies on education in Belgium, he continues his work as an education activist, campaigning for education for all as the 'great equalizer'.

Fiona Carnie is a Visiting Research Associate at the Institute of Education, University of London. She is currently working in the fields of Student Voice and Parent Voice. Her books, *Alternative Approaches to Education* (Routledge Falmer, 2003) and *Pathways to Child Friendly Schools* (Human Scale Education, 2004), explore ways of involving key stakeholders such as parents and young people in shaping educational provision. Fiona is Vice President of the European Forum for Freedom in Education www.effe-eu.org.

Gina Mumba Chiwela has been working as Programme Development Manager with the Peoples Action Forum, Zambia, since 1994. She has particular responsibility for training adult learning facilitators in the Reflect approach, policy research and advocacy and HIV/AIDS programmes. She led the programme on participatory school governance, an initiative to bring communities into active participation in the planning and management for schools. Gina currently represents the Reflect Network in Zambia on the PAMOJA Council that oversees the Africa Reflect Network.

Sue Cox is a Senior Lecturer at the University of East Anglia in the School of Education and Lifelong Learning where she teaches on postgraduate initial and continuing teacher education courses and undertakes research. Her particular area of interest is primary education (including philosophy of education, art and design education and citizenship education) and her research has included projects with children and teachers in primary schools on children's participation and decision-making.

Lynn Davies is Professor of International Education in the Centre for International Education and Research, University of Birmingham. Her main interests are in education and conflict (the contribution of schools to peace and to conflict), and in education for democracy (pupil voice, school councils). She is also working in the area of education and violent extremism, and her book *Educating Against Extremism* (2008) is being used by educationists and governments in the UK and beyond.

Rohit Dhankar is Secretary of the Indian non-government organization Diganter, of which he is a co-founder. A curriculum expert, he has served on the Government of India's National Curriculum Framework advisory team and currently teaches on the MA in Elementary Education at the Tata Institute of Social Sciences, Mumbai.

Caroline Dyer is a linguist by training and works at the Leeds University Centre for International Development, where she lectures in development practice. Her research interests focus on early years and adult literacy, and the educational inclusion of nomadic and migrant groups; she has authored numerous papers on these topics, and in 2006 edited an international volume on the *Education of Nomadic Peoples: current issues, future prospects* (Berghahn Books).

Notes on Contributors

Allan Fowler is a former high school teacher turned researcher who has taught for over 35 years in comprehensive education. He now works part-time for the Open University.

Clive Harber is Professor of International Education at the University of Birmingham. He was previously Head of the School of Education at the University of Birmingham and the University of Natal in Durban, South Africa. He has a long-standing international research interest in both education for democracy and its opposites.

Karen Lindridge has been a primary school teacher for twenty years and has taught all age groups from 4 [pre-school] to 11. She is currently Deputy Head at Old Bexley Church of England Primary School, Bexley. In addition, she spent three years as a teacher trainer at the University of Greenwich where she specialized in early years and physical education. She is currently interested in the area of providing children with opportunity and empowerment, which includes her involvement in the area of children as researchers.

P J Lolichen heads the Centre for Applied Research and Documentation at The Concerned for Working Children, Bangalore, India. He has been spearheading rights-based information management by children for the past 12 years and is a recipient of the MacArthur Fellowship for Leadership Development. His most recent publication is 'Taking a Right Turn: Children Lead the Way in Research', and he has published other works on information management by children, enabling their participation in governance.

Daniela Mamaliga has been *EveryChild Moldova*'s Programme Director since 2004. She joined *EveryChild Moldova* in 2001, initially as their Press Officer, becoming Project Coordinator and then Programme Director. Prior to that, Daniela worked for the government news agency *Moldpress*.

Esmeranda Manful is a Research Associate at the Centre for Research in Social Policy, Loughborough University. Her interests include children's rights, particularly the interpretation of the concept to improve the welfare of children.

Tristan McCowan is Lecturer in Education and International Development at the Institute of Education, University of London. His current research focuses on education and citizenship in Latin America.

Colin Richards is Emeritus Professor at the University of Cumbria and has been a senior HMI and a visiting professor at the Universities of Warwick, Leicester and Newcastle.

Anna Robinson-Pant is Reader at the Centre for Applied Research in Education, University of East Anglia, where her research has included projects with children and teachers in Norfolk schools, as well as with international students studying at the university. For around ten years, she worked in education, research and development with various NGOs in Nepal. Publications include: *Why Eat Green Cucumber at the Time of Dying? Exploring the Link between Women's Literacy and Development: A Nepal Perspective* (Unesco IOE, 2001), *Women, Literacy and Development: Alternative Perspectives* (Routledge, 2004) and *Cross-cultural Perspectives on Educational Research* (Open University Press, 2006).

Payal Saksena joined *EveryChild India* in 2008 as their Advocacy and Communications Manager. Before this, Payal worked for four years as a gender and law consultant for Global Rights: Partners for Justice, a US-based organization implementing an 'Access to Justice' project in Karnataka and Rajasthan in India.

Michele Schweisfurth is Reader in Comparative and International Education, and Director of the Centre for International Education and Research at the University of Birmingham. CIER's 'Educating for Global Justice' theme reflects her research interests. She is also joint editor of the journal *Comparative Education*.

Anne-Marie Smith is Postdoctoral Teaching Fellow at Liverpool Hope University, where she teaches in Childhood and Youth Studies. She previously worked as Children's Partipation coordinator at Liverpool World Centre. Her research with displaced children in Mexico has been published in *Children, Youth and Environments* (2007).

Doug Springate, now retired from the University of Greenwich, has teaching experience in primary and secondary schools and was a teacher trainer for the primary age phase for more than thirty years, lecturing in four institutions, including an American university. He was a Primary Ofsted Inspector. He has considerable international experience and is ex-chairman of ETEN, the European Teacher Education Network. He is currently further exploring the primary school as a democracy and researching and promoting the area of 'Children as Researchers', including an European Community funded project with institutions from seven European countries.

Liz Trippett worked for *EveryChild UK* as the Programme Officer for Asia, South America and the Caribbean for three years until October 2008. She currently works in a psychiatric hospital in the UK with children and adolescents experiencing mental health problems.

Lionel Vigil has been *EveryChild Peru*'s Programme Manager since March 2008. Prior to that, Lionel worked for *Management Science for Health Inc.* in Peru as a Programme Manager for a USAID-funded community health project, for the Peruvian NGO, PRISMA, and for the Peruvian Ministries of Health and Education.

Chris Williams is based at the Centre for International Education and Research (CIER), University of Birmingham. He has also held posts at the universities of London, Cambridge, Cairo, and the United Nations. His engagement in global justice and participation includes: street-working children in South Africa, Turkey, Lebanon and Afghanistan; disability rights in Britain, Egypt, China, Thailand and Japan; environmental victims in India; cultural diversity in Korea; and education for all in Palestine and Liberia.

Hiromi Yamashita is Research Fellow at the Centre for International Education and Research (CIER), University of Birmingham, which engages in research and teaching in the areas of global justice. Hiromi's interests include issues of participation (at all ages), democratic decision-making, environmental risk communication, sustainable development and global citizenship.

Introduction

Sue Cox, Caroline Dyer, Anna Robinson-Pant and
Michele Schweisfurth

Since the United Nations Convention on the Rights of the Child came into force in 1990, there has been an increasing recognition that, globally, children need to have more input into decisions concerning their own education. Researchers, activists, policy makers, international and national non-governmental organizations (NGOs) and educational institutions have been looking at ways of promoting children's involvement in decision-making. This book explores how children can, and do, actively participate in decision-making. It brings together perspectives from developed and developing countries,[1] with the aim of extending the current debates on children's participation by engaging a range of researchers and practitioners with differing practical agendas, philosophical orientations, and methodological approaches.

At the heart of questions over what decisions children should make, and how and when, is how we conceptualize children, their abilities and their rights. The UN Convention itself stipulates that the views of children need to be given due weight in accordance with their age and maturity (Article 12). But the age at which children are believed to be ready to make serious decisions that affect them and their education is open to interpretation, and these beliefs changes over time and across contexts. We would argue that it is important to go beyond token decision-making at an early stage, to give children a true sense of agency in their own lives, and not only to rehearse for adulthood. Several of the contributors to this book draw on Hart's (1992) 'ladder of participation' to analyse the purpose and ways in which children participate in decision-making. The ladder helps to distinguish different levels of children's input, ranging from the minimal end of manipulation and tokenism, through children being consulted while adults take the initiative, to the highest level of youth initiatives in which they decide how far to include adults. As many of the case studies in this book will show, it is usually adults who decide whether children can make decisions, and which children qualify.

As the agenda approaches the level of policy, in particular, adults are increasingly likely to be in control. Yet, as illustrated in this book, the benefits of children's decision-making to themselves and to schools and other organizations are multiple.

Schools have the potential to be sites of power for children, but they can also be, and often are, sites of repression. Many educators do not feel comfortable with allowing children's decisions in areas where power relations might shift as a result. Equally, the virtually universal standards agenda, with its focus on the 'basics' of literacy and numeracy, may not help to encourage the development of the less obviously scholastic skills of self-confidence and critical questioning that need to be fostered if children's involvement in decision-making is to grow.

It is interesting that while most of the UK-based chapters in this book refer to schools, many of the contributions from developing countries refer to NGO actions and other non-formal sites of education. This raises questions about whether it is best to work from within or outside the formal school system, and from within a set of cultural norms, or from a more cosmopolitan perspective. When considering the possibilities and limits of children's decision-making powers in different contexts, should local cultures and practices set the agenda, or are we working toward a shared set of goals bounded by a global moral framework? If the latter, how should this framework be negotiated, and is it realistic to apply it to institutions so different from each other?

The book is based on an Economic and Social Research Council-funded seminar series held at the Universities of East Anglia, Birmingham and Leeds during 2006–7. The seminars broke new ground in bringing together educators, researchers and activists working in a range of countries to present papers, discuss practice, and form collaborations. The chapters are based on papers presented, and the book seeks to develop the themes explored in the seminars and to present case studies of children involved in decision-making internationally. It does not do so uncritically, and the barriers to their participation are also explored.

The book is divided into four parts. The chapters in Part 1 ask, in various ways, whether we can make space for children's decision-making. They focus on the macro level of policy and how this is a starting point for practice. Policy includes that of national government, but also regional bodies and the work of international NGOs. Case studies include England, Brazil and the Philippines. From policy we move to practice: the chapters in Part 2 explore how children's decision-making affects practice in schools, communities and beyond, and the authors offer insights from Nepal, Zambia, Peru, India, Moldova, and the UK In Part 3, we consider the social and political dimensions of children as decision makers, asking what we are trying to achieve in terms of political agendas and social integration, equity, and citizenship. Along with further chapters from UK contexts, there are papers exploring these issues in Mexico and India. Finally, Part 4 asks how we facilitate children's participation. It draws mainly on experiences of children as researchers, as well as other forms of decision-making, providing perspectives from India and the UK on the question.

In the closing chapter of the book, as editors we adopt a comparative perspective to investigate what these cases from different national and cultural contexts tell us about children as decision makers, and what some of the facilitators and barriers are to fuller and more meaningful participation. We hope that this cross-cultural view will help to inform debate internationally – and that children will be included in the debate.

Notes

[1] We have chosen to use these terms rather than North/South or First/Third World, reflecting the preference of most of our contributing authors.

References

Hart, R. (1992) *Children's Participation: From Tokenism to Citizenship*, Innocenti Essays No. 4. Florence: UNICEF International Child Development Centre.

Part 1

Can we make space for children's decision-making? Perspectives on educational policy

Globally, attitudes to children have changed over time, towards acknowledging the importance of their decision-making. This is reflected, for example, in the almost universal ratification of the United Nations Convention on the Rights of the Child. Among the decision-making rights upheld by the Convention are children's right to stay with their parents if they choose (Article 9.1); to express their views freely (Article 13.1); and to assemble peacefully (Article 15.1). We would hope to see such shifts in attitude, and such international agreements, reflected in national policy and, in turn, in how these policies are enacted in schools, classrooms and other educational sites. The chapters in this part of the book explore how far, in different contexts, these aspirations are manifested; they also introduce concepts which facilitate analysis of children's involvement at different levels. Among the themes are the extent to which policy rhetoric is matched by reality, and the roles of organizations such as non-governmental organizations (NGOs) in bridging gaps and supporting children and adults in making children's decisions heard and realized. Policy can be an enabler, but it certainly does not guarantee that children are empowered, and, as some of these chapters point out, evidence of resistance can be found at many levels.

An historical overview of the situation in the England since 1965 provides an interesting case study of some of these themes. The intersection of politics and education creates a fluctuating trajectory. Rather than being taken seriously, Colin Richards argues that children's decision-making is restricted by such factors as high-stakes examinations and school league tables, driven by a performativity agenda. Increasingly, there are moves to include children's perspectives, for example in how their views of their schools and teachers are now part of the Office for Standards in Education (Ofsted) process of inspection, but 'myths' live on. Along with 'myths', Richards uses 'ages' and 'autonomy' as organizing ideas in his analysis, which is based on many years of experience with Ofsted and as an academic educationist observing policy and practice in England. We invite readers to compare his observations with the situation in other contexts.

Given the limitations of policy, organizations promoting children's right to decide have used interventionist tactics to facilitate the prerequisite skills, structures and attitudes. The following two chapters document case studies of such strategies, in different national contexts. In Chapter 2, Tristan McCowan considers the 'prefigurative' potential of schools in the Brazilian context, in relation to pupil participation in schools and ultimately in society. In particular, he analyses a municipal government's 'Plural School' initiative, based on the principle of inclusion through democratization. Once again, we find the challenges of facilitating the participation of all children, of democratizing the relationships between teachers and pupils, and of taking young people's decision-making powers beyond the more trivial elements of uniforms and food. However, there is evidence that the prefigurative strategies employed can lead to wider exercising of the right to participate.

The work of the international NGO Oxfam in conflict zones is the basis for the next chapter. Drawing on experience from conflict zones internationally, the region of Central Mindanao in the Philippines becomes the focus of an exploration of how conflict and poverty affect schooling and create particular conditions for the participation of children. Sheila Aikman considers how school as a place and as a social space can create opportunities, and how the dynamics of power affect processes. Among the achievements of the programme in Mindanao are higher levels of attendance, interest and participation from children, and fewer interruptions to schooling as a result of the conflict.

Finally, Clive Harber draws on evidence from a wide range of contexts to argue that, on the whole, school children are not decision makers, and that policy and teacher education are parts of the problem. He brings together studies of pupils' views of schooling to illustrate the 'unfreedoms' inherent in the purposes and structures of schooling. Crucially, the chapter also synthesizes evidence of how very important listening to pupils and giving them power and responsibility are. We might expect this in terms of developing the capacity for democratic citizenship, but it proves to be excellent practice even using more conventional indicators of effectiveness such as examination outcomes and pupil discipline.

Chapter 1

The changing context of decision-making in English primary education: ages, myths and autonomy

Colin Richards

Introduction

This chapter discusses children as decision makers in the context of developments in English primary education. It cannot do justice to developments elsewhere, whether in other parts of the United Kingdom or overseas. It uses three organizing ideas – 'ages', 'myths' and 'autonomy' – as a way of outlining the changing context in which English primary schools have operated, primary teachers have taught and primary pupils have experienced their schooling over the forty years since the publication of the Plowden Report (Central Advisory Council for Education 1967). Very largely the story is one of adult decision-making, albeit in a changing context, with different sets of adults making different kinds of decisions at different times. It is a story in which children's perspectives are not so much consciously ignored as not really considered – either in policy, research or school decision-making. There are some signs that at long last those perspectives are being seen as important – at least at the level of rhetoric but only very patchily as yet at the level of practice. The lessons of English history (if it has lessons) are not all that hopeful. There is a need now to make that rhetoric a reality – forty years after the Plowden Report was published with the title *Children and* Their *Primary Schools*, with its assertion that 'At the heart of the educational process lies the child', with its slogan 'The child as agent of his own learning', but with its 500-page report providing no evidence that children had ever been consulted in its deliberations!

An age of excitement, 1965–74

The first period, 1965–74 is termed 'an *age* of excitement' – but this, of course, is an adult viewpoint – that of a teacher. Would children, had they been asked (which they were not), have seen it in similar terms?

Despite very real problems (very large class sizes by current standards, high staff turnover and the vestiges of the eleven-plus[1]) there was a sense of optimism in the system – captured in the upbeat style, messages and rhetoric of the Plowden Report itself. Primary education was expanding in terms of numbers of pupils, increases in resources and rising public and professional expectations. There was a sense of freedom (coupled with anxiety) over the removal of the restrictions on teacher initiative following the demise (in many areas) of selection. There was a rhetoric, too, of increased freedom for children to pursue their own needs and interests, though what research there was into primary classrooms (Boydell 1974) and my experience as a primary school teacher revealed in most cases either the continuance of overt teacher direction or an illusory freedom offered children to do what teachers thought was in the children's best interests – a kind of pseudo-progressivism where children were given neither the tools nor the opportunities for genuine decision-making over their own learning.

There arose the *myth* of a primary school revolution – founded to some degree on highly innovative practice in a small minority of schools but essentially the result of wishful thinking on the part of some child-centred educationalists who occupied prominent positions in local education authorities (LEAs) and initial teacher education (Richards 1980). Though mythical, these ideas added to the sense of interest and anticipation in working in a system where the children, the teachers and the system itself were perceived to be full of unrealized possibilities. Teachers enjoyed (albeit rather anxiously) *licensed autonomy*; they were trusted by politicians and parents alike to take professional decisions about both the content of the curriculum and the way it should be taught and assessed. A parallel licensed autonomy was not offered to children – this was not the golden age of children's decision-making that some nostalgic liberals fondly imagine!

An age of disillusionment, 1974–88

The period 1974–88 was very different – seen from an educationist's perspective. There was virtually no research into how children perceived or influenced their educational experience during this period, despite a number of major classroom observational research projects. This was an *age* of disillusionment – with the post-war democratic consensus, with the state of the British economy, with the condition of the public services, with the quality of primary education and with the standards achieved by primary school pupils. National surveys of primary and middle schools (Department of Education and Science 1978, 1983), classroom observational research (Galton et al. 1980) and my own personal experience visiting schools as a university lecturer and latterly as a government inspector revealed a substantial gap (inevitable to some degree) between professional rhetoric and practice, not least in relation to the degree of freedom accorded primary pupils – revealed as illusory despite the wild claims of populist rhetoric over teachers abdicating responsibility over teaching and learning to their pupils – as illustrated by publications such as the Black Papers (e.g. Cox and Boyson 1975, 1977) written by conservative academics, many with little direct experience of English state schools or pupils.

These factors, within and external to the educational system, helped establish a *myth* of decline, especially of declining standards in literacy and numeracy. Though decision-making over curriculum, teaching and assessment remained largely in the hands of schools (and, more particularly, of individual teachers), there was a loss of professional self-confidence and direction in the face of continuing criticism, despite the fact there was no substantial evidence either from research or school inspection of a decline in educational standards or of pupils being accorded excessive degrees of freedom. Teachers exercised a kind of *monitored autonomy*, as during the 1980s both central and local government began to develop policies for the curriculum and LEAs tried to monitor and influence practice in individual schools. However, the notion of pupil perspective, let alone pupil consultation or decision-making, featured in neither national nor LEA thinking.

An age of regulation, 1988–97

The next nine-year period can be characterized as an *age* of regulation. It would be interesting to know in what terms primary pupils experienced it, but the research was never undertaken. The stirrings of government involvement, begun in the previous period, were replaced by strong intervention especially in the areas of curriculum and assessment. For the first time since 1897 English primary schools were required to follow a detailed, codified, state-imposed curriculum and were provided with a national system of assessment successively modified over the years – there was little scope for decision-making by schools and teachers attempting to grapple with an overloaded, over-assessed curriculum. An attempt to introduce citizenship as a cross-curricular theme offered the possibility of pupil participation beyond the national curriculum, but like the other cross-curricular themes citizenship never got off the ground. There was one interesting counter-movement to note – the introduction of 'circle time' in a small number of schools – at last giving children something of a 'voice' but not usually involving decision-making of any substantial kind. For teachers, *regulated autonomy* replaced monitored autonomy. The instigation of a national cycle of inspection was a very powerful, though indirect, way of regulating the system – policing schools' compliance with national directives and severely limiting or even precluding high-risk experimentation with content, process or decision-making. The *myth* of low standards especially in the so-called 'basics' promulgated particularly by Ofsted's second chief inspector (see Richards 1997) was used to justify tighter regulation and control, though the evidence was, at worst, very suspect and, at best, far from conclusive.

An age of domination, 1997–2003

The first six years of the New Labour government can best be described as an *age* of domination; children may have experienced it in terms of tests, targets, plenaries and carpet-sitting! Far from restoring (albeit in a more accountable form) initiative and freedom to experiment in the primary sector, central government intervened ever more directly and sharply. It introduced a national literacy strategy which was far more detailed and prescriptive than the national curriculum orders ever were (see Wyse et al. 2008). The accompanying numeracy strategy provided rather more 'degrees of freedom' but only relative to its literacy equivalent. The government set early learning goals for the under-sixes. It prescribed teaching methods which were dangerously close to breaking the law as laid down in the 1988 Education Reform Act. It made a fetish of national testing – treating it as *the* measure for judging the performance of primary schools. It signally failed to curb the excesses of Ofsted and used that organization to reinforce the domination of the measurable and gradable as the expression of standards and quality. It was symptomatic of this period that pupils' views and perspectives never featured in any governmental consultation or inspection framework.

The government pursued the *myth* of modernization but paradoxically in a way more reminiscent of the nineteenth than the twenty-first century. Modernization was to be achieved through an unquestioning acceptance of government initiatives; there was 'zero tolerance' of dissent; criticism was treated as indicative of vested interests in 'old' (i.e. pre-1997) education which needed to be swept away or ignored. The government offered schools and teachers *rhetorical autonomy*; they were free in principle to opt out of initiatives such as the national strategies, but at their peril, given policing by Ofsted inspectors, LEA officers and government officials, all with anxious eyes on school, LEA and national targets.

There were, however, some interesting counter-initiatives. Though non-statutory (and receiving little other than rhetorical support from the Department for Education and Skills), personal, social, health and citizenship education was reintroduced. 'Circle time' became increasingly common (it is interesting to speculate why), notions of student voice were aired (especially in secondary schools) and the school council movement began to grow. Researchers became interested in children's perspectives, as illustrated by the Primary Assessment, Curriculum and Experience (PACE) project (Pollard and Triggs 2000; Osborn et al. 2000) which documented primary children's perceived loss of autonomy and increasing instrumental approach to schooling as they grew older amid the pressure of the dominant performativity regime.

An age of contradictions: from 2003 to the present

It is particularly difficult to characterize the current period – an *age* of emancipation? (hardly), an *age* of illusions? (possibly) or an *age* of contradictions? (most likely). But perhaps at long last we may have a better view of how children are experiencing it through their participation in school councils and in children-as-researcher projects.

In one sense surveillance remains a dominant theme. The national curriculum remains in place; the national tests still operate at the ages of 7 and 11; targets still dominate the educational landscape; performance tables show no sign of disappearing. A thousand pages of revised numeracy and literacy 'guidance' have been issued on-line. The government has made the teaching of synthetic phonics mandatory – in clear contradiction to the 1988 Education Reform Act and to a century of teacher autonomy over teaching methodology. Ofsted inspections continue – at more frequent intervals and with a supposedly 'lighter touch' but carrying the danger of constant surveillance as the psychological reality in schools.

Yet there are some countervailing developments. The government claims as its goal 'for every primary school to combine excellence in teaching with enjoyment of learning'. Through the primary national strategy, schools are being encouraged to be more innovative and creative and to use the increased 'freedom' to provide a more flexible curriculum (though the possible role of pupils in influencing that curriculum is unclear). Assessment *for* learning, including pupil self-assessment, is in favour (though not at the expense of national assessment *of* learning). *Every Child Matters* (Department for Education and Skills 2003) promises at long last joined-up thinking and joined-up services. Extended schools offer exciting possibilities (but are children being consulted, or even making decisions, as to the activities to be made available?). Two inquiries – one into the nature of childhood and one (the *Cambridge Primary Review*) reviewing the state of primary education –

have been undertaken, though not by the government; in both, children's views are being sought. Ofsted is at long last expecting schools to seek, and act on, the views of pupils. School councils are gaining ground; work with children as researchers is beginning to develop. The issue of children as decision makers is on the research agenda – but is it on schools' or the government's agenda?

It is not possible to offer a definitive guiding *myth* for this period, but it is possible that we may be witnessing a partial (but still precarious) *relicensed autonomy* for English teachers.

But what are we offering children forty years on from the Plowden Report? Are children at last to have a say in *their* primary schools? Through school councils and the like are we simply (but importantly) helping them to understand their future roles as citizens or are we helping them to develop here and now as participatory school citizens? What are the dilemmas, contradictions and methodological problems involved in developing that school citizenry, both in England and elsewhere? The rest of this book (with its cross-cultural case-studies) promises fascinating glimpses into such questions. What *age* might we be helping to usher in?

Notes

[1]   The eleven-plus examination was taken by children at the end of primary school, to determine eligibility for entry into selective secondary schools. Versions remain in place in some parts of the country.

References

Boydell, D. (1974) 'Teacher-pupil contact in junior classrooms', *British Journal of Educational Psychology*, 44, 313–18.

Central Advisory Council for Education (1967) *Children and Their Primary Schools*. London: HMSO.

Cox, C. B. and Boyson, R. (eds) *Black Paper 1975*. London: Dent.

Cox, C. B. and Boyson, R. (eds) *Black Paper 1977*. London: Temple Smith.

Department for Education and Science (1978) *Primary Education in England: A Survey by H M Inspectors of Schools*. London: HMSO.

Department of Education and Science (1983) *9–13 Middle Schools: An Illustrative Survey*. London: HMSO.

Department for Education and Skills (2003) *Every Child Matters: Change for Children*. Nottingham: DfES Publications.

Galton, M., Simon, B. and Croll, P. (1980) *Inside the Primary Classroom*. London: Routledge.

Osborn, M., McNess, E. and Broadfoot, P. (2000) *What Teachers Do: Changing Policy and Practice in Primary Education*. London: Continuum.

Pollard, A. and Triggs, P. (2000) *What Pupils Say: Changing Policy and Practice in Primary Education*. London: Continuum.

Richards, C. (1980) 'Demythologising primary education'. *Journal of Curriculum Studies*, 12(1).

Richards, C. (1997) *Primary Education, Standards and Ofsted: Towards a More Authentic Conversation*. Coventry: Centre for Research in Elementary and Primary Education, University of Warwick.

Wyse, D., McCreery, E. and Torrance, H. (2008) *The Trajectory and Impact of National Reform: Curriculum and Assessment in English Primary Schools*, Primary Review Research Survey 3/2. Cambridge: Cambridge Primary Review (University of Cambridge, Faculty of Education).

Chapter 2

'Prefigurative' approaches to participatory schooling: experiences in Brazil

Tristan McCowan

Recent interest in increasing pupil participation in school decision-making has had diverse motivations. Participation can be seen as a *right*, as enshrined in the 1989 United Nations Convention on the Rights of the Child. Yet there are a number of other instrumental justifications. Pupil participation has been linked to 'school effectiveness' and 'school improvement', increases in test scores, improvements in the behaviour of pupils, and enhancing the overall ethos of the school (Flutter and Ruddock 2004; Harber and Trafford 1999; Macbeath and Moos 2004).[1]

The rationales outlined above are characterized by an extrinsic value given to participation, in relation to the educational and other benefits it brings to individuals and institutions. However, participation can also be supported from the standpoint of its intrinsic democratic value. Democratic structures in schools, from this perspective, are a good in themselves, whether or not they contribute to the performance of students academically or socially. At the same time they may also be means by which students can develop knowledge, skills and values related to democratic participation outside the school.

This chapter explores participatory approaches to schooling based in an intrinsic valuing of democracy. Specifically, it focuses on the *prefigurative* approach. A case of school democratization in Brazil – the Plural School – is analysed in order to explore the possibilities of these prefigurative forms. While this experience encounters significant problems in relation to implementation, it represents an important instance of participatory approaches.

The notion of the 'prefigurative'

Boggs (1977–8) defines prefiguration as 'the embodiment, within the ongoing political practice of a movement, of those forms of social relations, decision-making, culture and human experience that are the ultimate goal'. Historically, prefigurative movements developed in opposition to forms of Marxism that looked to a revolution headed by a strong party as the most effective way of achieving the goal of the socialist society. In these consequentialist forms, the means were in tension with the ends, in that hierarchical organization and violence were used to achieve a peaceful, non-hierarchical society. In contrast, other forms of revolutionary organization aimed to embody the values of the desired society within their political activities. Prefigurative forms have been incorporated in a variety of forms of organization, but particularly in anarchist (e.g. Franks 2003) and feminist movements (e.g. Epstein 1991; Rowbotham 1979).

A key characteristic of the prefigurative is that it cannot simply be abandoned in favour of a more effective strategy, since it is not only a means but also an instantiation of the end in the present. It involves either a *harmony* between or a *unification* of ends and means (McCowan 2008). In addition, prefigurative forms are not only instrumental to the transformation of society, but also for personal liberation (Gordon 2007), providing important informal learning experiences for those involved, both individually and collectively. It is also possible for *formal* education to be prefigurative. Michael Fielding's (e.g. 1997, 2007) work on radical state schooling, for example, draws extensively on the idea of the prefigurative.

The Brazilian context

Brazil has a history of authoritarianism, and of extreme socio-economic inequalities. However, in the period following the military dictatorship of 1964–85, there has been a wave of democratization, and a number of inspiring civil society organizations and movements have emerged, particularly in the area of education (e.g. Gandin 2006; McCowan 2006; Myers 2008). The decentralized nature of the Brazilian system has meant that opposition to dominant paradigms has taken the form not only of pressuring central government for policy changes, but also of actively constructing alternatives at the local level. A number of significant local government initiatives have emerged in the last twenty years, many under municipal governments of the Workers' Party (*Partido dos Trabalhadores*, PT). The case discussed here, the Plural School, is a local initiative of this type.

The case study involved qualitative research carried out in 2005–6. In addition to a general overview, three schools were chosen for in-depth research. Interviews were conducted with three officials of the Municipal Secretariat of Education (Secretaria Municipal de Educação, SMED), and, in the focus schools, with the head-teacher, three classroom teachers, and three groups of students aged 13–17. Interviews were conducted and transcribed in Portuguese (quotations appearing in this chapter have been translated into English by the author). Classroom observations were also carried out, as well as documentary analysis involving official curriculum guidance and pedagogical materials at the school level.

There are many aspects of interest in this initiative, but this chapter will focus on approaches to pupil participation. The Plural School does not use the language of the 'prefigurative' explicitly, but clearly displays a commitment to this form of organization in both its writings and practice. First there will be an overview of the initiative, followed by an outline of its approach to pupil participation and assessment of its implementation in practice.

The Plural School

The Plural School (PS) is an initiative of the municipal government of Belo Horizonte, a large city with a metropolitan area of over 5 million inhabitants. The city is the capital of Minas Gerais, a relatively wealthy state, but one with severe inequalities, leaving a significant proportion of the population in poverty and political marginalization. A disproportionate part of this group is made up by the black and mixed-race communities, many descendants of the slaves who were brought to the region during the gold boom of the eighteenth century. Belo Horizonte's municipal system has some 164 primary and 26 secondary schools,[2] as well as pre-school, special education and youth and adult education provision (Instituto Nacional de Estudos e Pesquisas Educacionais Anísio Teixeira (INEP) 2007).

The PS, initiated in the 1990s, is a framework of policy and practice based around the principle of inclusion. In particular, the PS aims to combat 'school failure', represented by drop-out and grade repetition. The traditional school is seen to exclude sections of the community in a number of ways: through its choice of valued knowledge, its assessment procedures, the structure of the school day and the teacher–student relationship. The framework, therefore, represents an opening of this rigid system to a plurality of individuals, groups and cultures, giving each equal value and opportunity. The distinctive feature of the PS is its recognition that the realization of the right to education can be a form of exclusion if attention is not paid to processes and experiences within the school. Implementation of this vision, however, is not without challenges. Existing research (e.g. Dalben 2000; Glória and Mafra 2004) shows these difficulties, particularly in relation to misunderstanding of and resistance to the initiative by teachers, students and the local communities.

Addressing school democratization

The importance of pupil participation in the PS framework is shown in the following statement by SMED (2002: 15): 'All [the politico-pedagogical plans] propose the development of the citizen for participation in society. All these proposals note that school will develop these collective subjects in as far as they make them participants in the construction of humanized school spaces.'

The development of democratic citizenship, therefore, depends on the democratic culture prefigured in the schools. There are a number of bodies in which pupils participate. The School Assembly, with the participation of the whole school community, has the function of making decisions on key issues such as arrangements during a teachers' strike. The smaller School Council (clearly distinct from that seen in the UK), with student, teacher and community representatives, has a more executive role, with responsibilities including management of the budget. While there are federal, state and municipal guidelines on the curriculum, individual schools have a large degree of leeway regarding what is taught. Schools, therefore, construct their own distinctive 'politico-pedagogical plans', which provide the basis for the curriculum. Direct elections for head-teachers are also universal, aiming to make school leadership more responsive to local needs and political demands. The participation of students, therefore, takes place in the context of a wider democratic basis for schooling, involving teachers and communities as well.

The *grêmios* are another key site for pupil participation. These are pupil associations, elected by the pupils themselves, which organize cultural, sporting and political activities in the school and act as a forum for discussion and as a mouthpiece for student views. These have a long history in Brazilian schools, yet the municipal government has aimed to give them impetus, and particularly to enhance their political function.

A key aspect of the participatory culture in PS schools, and one which serves to differentiate it from some other efforts at school democratization, is that it is embedded within a commitment to transforming political relations. This is contained particularly in the adherence to Freirean dialogue as a pedagogical principle. Dialogue, in the Freirean sense, involves a radical alteration of the relations between teacher and student, and of the process of knowledge construction and acquisition (Freire 1972).

The PS approach, therefore, is one in which the specific opportunities for pupil participation in decision-making – such as the School Council and *grêmio* – are underpinned by a commitment to democratic teacher-student relations and Freirean dialogue.

Challenges of implementation

While there were a number of structures through which students could participate, the *grêmio* was the most prominent in the data. Those students strongly engaged in the *grêmios* reported significant political development. Thaís,[3] a *grêmio* leader, described the process of broadening her understanding of political issues as a result of her participation:

> The *grêmio* campaigns for things for the school. For example, you see there is a teacher missing. Ah! You complain to the head. But it is not the fault of the head that there is a teacher missing, that the desks are broken, that there are not enough materials. It is a national problem. You begin to see that the structure of society is much bigger. So you begin to get involved in larger issues than this, not only in the *grêmio*.

However, while students like Thaís had very rich processes of political development, they are not representative of the whole pupil body. Students who did not participate directly in the *grêmio* associated it principally with organizing parties and excursions and expressed scepticism about its political nature, and its efficacy in giving a voice to student views.

As well as difficulties in extending participation to all within the school, there were also divergences between schools. At one school, the *grêmio* was almost non-existent:

> TM: Is there a *grêmio* in the school?
>   . . .
> Pupil 1:   Ah. I've heard there is, though I've never seen it.
>   . . .
> Pupil 2:   There is a *grêmio*, but I've never seen their proposals, there isn't even an election. . ..
> Pupil 3:   You see, they organized a time for meeting that was only convenient for the organizing group, it wasn't for other people in the school.

However, taking a perspective broader than participation in the *grêmio*, there was evidence of a general increase in student participation in decision-making. Dora, a deputy head, believed strongly that the students in her school had undergone a process of political empowerment. She emphasized the link between democratic processes in the school and political participation outside it, between the prefigurative and the prefigured:

> So I see that a good proportion of our students manage to understand and live that democracy and then live it outside. Because if it is lived in the school ... if he [*sic*, the pupil] manages to participate in the life of the

school where he is seen as a citizen with rights, he can exercise these rights here in the school, and that implies duties too. For him it seems clear to have that role outside, to be an aware citizen.

Student action was often restricted to deciding relatively trivial elements of school rules, such as their not wearing uniforms, and being able to leave the school at lunchtimes. Yet at times it also extended to the curriculum. Segundo pointed to the empowerment of his students to critique his own teaching:

> So they have a strong critique of my classes. So if I enter into any contradiction, they stop me there and then, something that I think is great...because I see that they contest things, they don't accept passively everything that I say ... [B]ecause often the pupil sees the teacher as the master of knowledge.

Even three students who were not active participants in the *grêmio* emphasized the change in power relations:

TM: Do you think in general the voice of the student is heard?
Pupil 1:   It has more weight than the voice of the teacher I think.
Pupil 2:   Yes, it's because the students are in the majority.... one or
             other voice doesn't count for much, but the voice of the
             people I think it has more power than the voice of the
             teachers themselves, of the head-teacher.
Pupil 3:   And also we can demand things, what we want, we can ask
             for our rights, you see.
TM: And do you manage it?
Pupil 2:   We even get rid of teachers who aren't teaching properly.

While the pupils have perhaps overstated their influence in relation to teachers here, the key point is the *perception* of their right to power in the school. Not surprisingly, teachers were a little nervous about this growing student influence, and about the evaluations of them that the students were beginning to carry out in some schools.

Another important aspect of the initiative related to gender, with the disparities of political influence in the wider society to a large extent overcome. Girls were more prominent than boys as representatives in decision-making bodies (such as the *grêmio*), and had female role models not only in relation to classroom teachers but also in positions of responsibility in school and local authority.

So, while participation in the *grêmios* may have been limited, there was evidence of a significant shift in power relations in the schools, and empowerment of the students. In addition to processes within the school, there were instances of direct political participation outside:

> We worked in a building much worse than this ... the children mobilized themselves, a group of teachers and pupils ... . They went to the street, they closed off the street, there were politicians there, there was a really strong participation and afterwards ... we managed to get the funds through the participatory budget from the city council.
>
> (Interview with the head-teacher Ermenegilda)

Student campaigning was also instrumental in getting soundproofing from traffic noise for the school. Another campaign was mounted in order to make up the shortfall in teachers. This protest led to students being arrested, and the consequent publicity put pressure on the SMED, who on the very next day provided extra teachers. Dora said in relation to this incident: 'Have they had a better citizenship class? I think they haven't.'

In summary, there was evidence of widespread democratization of the schools in question, with students becoming more aware of their rights and able to articulate them. In formal structures such as the *grêmio*, however, participatory experiences were very rich for some, but limited to a small number of people, and there was a disparity in the introduction of these bodies across the school system. Importantly, participation in the school context led on to political action outside.

Implications of a prefigurative experience

The experience outlined above has highlighted some important questions in relation to pupil participation in schools. Firstly, it seems vital that representative bodies for pupils are embedded in a deeper democratization, involving fundamental aspects of teacher–student relations and decision-making over teaching and learning, in conjunction with participatory structures for teachers and the local community. This is important in order to avoid fragmented instances of pupil participation leading to trivialization and tokenism. It is also important that democratic experiences within the school are linked to wider political action outside it.

The case explored here illustrates the aspects of prefigurative forms identified above. It is an instantiation of an inclusive, democratic society, and also a site for learning, through the experiencing of these new forms of relation, and the development of knowledge, skills and values for participation. Lastly, it is an example of how alternatives can function in practice, providing lessons and inspiration for others.

However, as shown above, the initiative is not without its problems. There is always a risk of representative bodies channelling student demands towards unthreatening areas such as recreation times and clothing, rather than curriculum and management. Increases in pupil influence also threaten the positions of teachers, who can serve – either actively or by default – to dampen down the changes. Nevertheless, they serve to illustrate an orientation for pupil participation that goes beyond tokenistic forms and instrumental, non-democratic rationales.

A number of complex questions, however, are raised by the fact that prefigurative forms exist within wider social contexts that at best are unsupportive, and at worst, hostile to them. It is not clear how well equipped the students from the Plural School will be to face the anti-democratic and exclusionary wider society. A further question arises in terms of the viability of initiating these educational forms in other contexts. Brazil is a country of extreme socio-economic inequalities and injustices, but it does allow space for the creation of educational and political alternatives at the local level. It is unclear whether similar initiatives could emerge in more stifling conditions. Nevertheless, a commitment to the prefigurative means that attempts must always be made to construct new forms of living in the here and now, rather than waiting for social transformation at some point in the future.

Notes

[1] It is not being suggested that the authors cited here necessarily endorse these rationales, only that these works illustrate them.

[2] Primary school in Brazil is usually of 8 years' duration, corresponding officially to the 7–14 age group. Secondary school is only for 3 years, for ages 15–17.

[3] Pseudonyms have been used for all individuals.

References

Boggs, C. (1977–8) 'Marxism, prefigurative communism, and the problem of workers' control'. *Radical America*, 11(6) and 12(1).

Dalben, A. I. L. de F. (ed.) (2000) *Avaliaçao da Implementação do Projeto Político-Pedagógico Escola Plural*. Belo Horizonte: GAME/FaE/UFMG.

Epstein, B. (1991) *Political Protest and Cultural Revolution: Nonviolent Direct Action in the 1970s and 1980s*. Berkeley, University of California Press.

Fielding, M. (1997) 'Beyond school effectiveness and school improvement: lighting the slow fuse of possibility'. *Curriculum Journal*, 8(1).

Fielding, M. (2007), 'On the necessity of radical state education: democracy and the common school'. *Journal of Philosophy of Education*, 41(4).

Flutter, J. and Ruddock, J. (2004) *Consulting Pupils: What's in it for Schools?* London: RoutledgeFalmer.

Franks, B. (2003), 'Direct action ethic'. *Anarchist Studies*, 11(1).

Freire, P. (1972) *Pedagogy of the Oppressed*. London: Sheed and Ward.

Gandin, L. A. (2006) 'Creating real alternatives to neo-liberal policies in education: The citizen school project', in M. W. Apple and K. Buras (eds), *The Subaltern Speak: Curriculum, Power, and Educational Struggles*. New York: Routledge.

Glória, D. M. A. and Mafra, L. de A. (2004) A prática da não-retenção escolar na narrativa de professores do ensino fundamental: dificuldades e avanços na busca do sucesso escolar, *Educação e Pesquisa*, 30(2).

Gordon, U. (2007) 'Anarchism reloaded'. *Journal of Political Ideologies*, 12(1).

Harber, C. and Trafford, B. (1999) 'Democratic management and school effectiveness in two countries: a case of pupil participation?' *Educational Management and Administration*, 27(1).

INEP (2007) Edudatabrasil. http://www.edudatabrasil.inep.gov.br (accessed 15 August 2007).

Macbeath, J. and Moos, L. (2004) *Democratic Learning: the Challenge of School Effectiveness*. London: RoutledgeFalmer.

McCowan, T. (2006) 'Educating citizens for participatory democracy: a case study of local government education policy in Pelotas, Brazil'. *International Journal of Educational Development*, 26(5).

McCowan, T. (2008) 'Curricular transposition in citizenship education' *Theory and Research in Education*, 6(2).

Myers, J. (2008) 'Democratizing school authority: Brazilian teachers' perceptions of the election of principals'. *Teaching and Teacher Education*, 24.

Rowbotham, S. (1979) *Beyond the Fragments*. London: Merlin.

Secretaria Municipal de Educação (2002) *II Congresso Político-Pedagógico da Rede Municipal de Ensino/Escola Plural* (3rd edn). Belo Horizonte: SMED.

Chapter 3

Grasping rare moments for change: children's participation in conflict contexts

Sheila Aikman

Introduction

This chapter examines the challenges of promoting children's participation and decision-making in schools in situations of chronic conflict and poverty. It arises from discussions with Oxfam Great Britain (GB) colleagues from Liberia, the Democratic Republic of the Congo and the Philippines on developing strategies to promote quality education in post-conflict and chronic conflict contexts. In particular, it takes Oxfam GB's education programme in the conflict-affected region of Central Mindanao in the Philippines as a starting point for broader reflection on the possibilities for participation. This development programme aims to transform schools into democratic, safe and responsive learning environments for healing and peace-building through working with children, parents and teachers.[1] The chapter draws on dimensions of Gaventa's (2006) power cube to investigate the nature of the challenge of fostering the school as an enabling place and democratic space for young people's decision-making.

The chapter begins by examining the characteristics of schools and schooling in contexts affected by long-term conflict and poverty. It explores decision-making as a particular kind of participation and examines forms of power and power relations that shape what is possible in classrooms and school. It then discusses the nature of opportunities for transformatory change and multidimensional strategies needed.

Schooling in contexts of chronic poverty and conflict

This exploration is shaped by my work with Oxfam GB and its educational programmes in the conflict and chronic conflict contexts of Sudan, the

Democratic Republic of the Congo, Liberia and Mindanao in the Philippines. It is the length and intensity of the conflict which links these countries as well as the inter-generational poverty experienced by people in the conflict zones.[2] In these and other countries, or regions within countries, which have experienced long periods of war, there are huge needs for rebuilding in terms of protecting children, preventing conflict and being an entry point for social reconstruction and economic and political change (International Save the Children Alliance 2006; Smith 2004; Tawil and Harley 2004).

Education is firmly recognized as a right and investment in schooling as an instrumental good for the development of a new generation of young people who can determine and shape a democratic and peaceful society. In post-conflict Liberia, Conneh (2008) lays out the expectations for schooling to address not only economic poverty and destitution but also vulnerability, illiteracy and violent masculinities. These are huge demands for schooling in any context. Rebuilding the education sector and ensuring that schools are running often means starting from very little. After conflict in which lives may have been threatened, rights abused, social norms disregarded, sexual violence rife and children's rights disrespected, schools, where they exist at all, can be bleak shells of buildings devoid of resources, with both the young people they serve and the teachers who work in them struggling to survive lives of abject poverty.

But, as Harber reminds us in Chapter 4 of this book, even in the absence of war and open conflict, schooling for young people living in chronic poverty can be a bleak experience and far from propitious for young people's decision-making, though there are always exceptions.

Chronic conflict in Mindanao

Schools are not easily transformed into the kind of institutions able to meet expectations for social renewal and transformation. Yet this is the aim of Oxfam GB's current education work in Mindanao.[3]

The island of Mindanao in the Philippine archipelago has experienced chronic conflict over centuries with cycles of conflict over the past thirty years, leading to periods of large-scale displacement, the most recent being in 2000 and 2003, with unrest in 2006 and an upsurge in violence again in 2008. The conflict is complex and rooted in political, economic, religious and cultural factors affecting the mixed population of Muslim, Christian and Lumad indigenous people. This mostly agricultural region has seen little or no growth in the economy or investment in institutions or basic services for many decades, and national expenditure on education has been declining. Indeed, educational levels in Mindanao are low compared to other provinces, with only three in every five children enrolled in school and of these only three in every ten reaching grade 6 of primary schooling. When conflict breaks out schooling is interrupted and schools may be either destroyed or used as evacuation centres; either way they cease to function as schools and many children drop out for good (Oxfam GB 2002, 2005).

In the conflict zone in Mindanao schools are an important community institution at the local level and serve as an entry point for resources and support during and after emergencies. In 2001 a programme was developed which went beyond previous emergency support for reconstructing buildings and supplying educational materials, working with partner organizations[4] to promote the UNICEF concept of 'child-friendly schools'. More recently, Oxfam and partners have broadened and deepened their approach and are implementing a programme entitled Partnership in Education for Community Empowerment (Oxfam GB 2006). Through reform of schools, and supporting and training a new generation of caring teachers, the programme set out to transform schools into places able to protect children from violence and the fear of violence, respect their rights, promote new and deepening forms of democracy and become a beacon for wider community change. The Mindanao programme came about because different actors – non-governmental organizations (NGOs), local communities and government – identified the school as providing an opportunity and space for change and saw young people as the catalysts for peace-building beyond its walls. In its approach it is strengthening the school as a place for peace and learning, classrooms as social spaces for democratic and peaceful relationships, and drawing on a consensus that radical change is needed to break decades of conflict and deepening poverty.

Decision-making as active participation – the potential of the school

The Mindanao programme's aims, therefore, are concerned with transforming school ethos, relationships and culture to make it a space for developing young people's self-esteem and confidence, their participation and the development of tolerance and cooperation. These aims find resonance in a broad definition of participation by the Department for Education and Skills (2004, quoted in Davies et al. 2005): 'Pupil participation, in practice, means opening up opportunities for decision-making with children and young people as partners engaging in dialogue, conflict resolution, negotiation and compromise – all important life skills.'

But there are many definitions of participation. The Minimum Standards for Education in Emergencies (Inter-Agency Network for Education in Emergencies (INEE) 2004) flag up the importance of children's participation in education activities and their right to a say in matters affecting their lives, as well as involvement in the development and management of the system providing their education. Thomson and Holdsworth (2003, cited in Davies et al. 2005) view participation as a continuum moving from 'being physically present' through increasing degrees of engagement to 'social activism': from passively 'taking part' to actively having a 'voice', being listened to and having decisions acted upon. Engaging in dialogue, being a decision maker and working towards conflict resolution are activities associated with 'active' forms of participation.

Goetz and Gaventa (2001) look at potentials for citizen voice and degrees of public sector responsiveness. They highlight different steps in moving citizen voice from access to presence and influence. They are concerned with understanding power dynamics and who has the power and capacity to exercise agency and realize the potential of rights, citizenship or voice (Gaventa 2006: 24). What kinds of participation do young people need to 'use their right to have a say in matters affecting their own lives' (INEE 2004: 17)?

It is argued here that to achieve the ambitious goal of young people's active participation in and through the school in chronic poverty- and conflict-affected contexts means addressing change in three dimensions: the school as a place; the school as a space for democratic relationships; and the school as an opportunity for wider social transformation.

The first dimension, the school as a place, is concerned with whether young people have access to functioning schools. What is the potential for children's voice in decision-making about design and location of schools, teachers' attendance and allocation of resources for materials? Are they able to negotiate schooling in relation to demands placed on them from home for their labour, and how is spending of scarce resources prioritized when schooling implies costs such as fees, uniforms, transport and school materials? And should schools provide meals? Are there mechanisms for young people to participate in such discussions? And if there are, are they merely there are spectators or are they able to influence? Are they tolerated as 'children' or listened to as young people with a diversity of perspectives and opinions?

The second dimension is about the kind of social space that exists in the classroom and school, what freedoms it offers young people and what kind of social ethos the school promotes. This involves working with teachers, head-teachers and school management for the implementation of teaching and learning practices embedded in facilitatory approaches, and relationships based on respect for young people as individuals and recognition of their diversity, be this ethnic identity, religious affiliation or linguistic difference. It implies responsiveness to young people's experience of violence and insecurity – and understanding that teachers themselves may need psychosocial support. What mechanisms exist for children's decision-making in school management and governance, and how do such representative structures need to be developed?

The third dimension is that of opportunity. What kind of opportunities does the school offer for allowing young people to be active agents in shaping critical areas of schooling such as what knowledge is valued in the curriculum and the learning materials, whose language is recognized in the classroom, and what kind of teaching and learning and evaluation processes are agreed to be free from discrimination or bias? It is about bringing young people's engagement to a point where they can translate access and presence into a tangible impact on policy-making and the organization of service delivery (Goetz and Gaventa 2001). For many education systems this would be seen as radical challenge as the curriculum and syllabus are nationally developed and disseminated, with a view to ensuring homogeneity, unity and nation-building. Those who are used to making these decisions may not be willing to share their power. The Mindanao programme has been providing out-of-school opportunities for young people to come together on a wide range of issues and concerns ranging from peace-building to climate change. Young Muslim women are engaging in an active and confident way not seen before (A. Pura, personal communication, September 2008).

Participation and the dynamics of power

The Mindanao programme has supported the development of the school as a functioning and welcoming place for learning, valued by students, teachers and parents alike. The programme is also engaged in ongoing work with young people, teachers and the community to develop these schools as spaces for tolerance and cooperation through dialogue and negotiation which in turn can contribute to building a peaceful and democratic society. Furthermore, it is using this space and the processes and systems of schooling to support young people to be agents of change and influence decisions over their own education and lives. These different dimensions of change, discussed above, provide a challenging agenda. As Kabeer (2002) reminds us, the project of constructing more inclusive forms of citizenship, be this through the school or other entry points, is not amenable to quick-fix solutions and we need to understand what factors explain continuities of exclusion and what lead to change. An analysis of forms and dynamics of power can provide insights into how inequalities, vulnerability and marginalization are perpetuated or overcome: 'The most commonly recognized form of power, power over, has many negative associations for people, such as repression, force, coercion, discrimination and abuse. At its most basic, it operates to privilege certain people while marginalising others'. Power also works in different ways – visible, hidden and invisible (Miller et al. 2006). Mapping power and recognizing its different manifestations is important for understanding how to develop effective strategies for achieving change.

In relation to the school and schooling we can view visible power in terms of formal decision-making mechanisms such as rules, regulations and structures of education authorities and institutions. Hidden power is wielded by actors who may not be formal decision makers, such as government officials or school governance bodies, but gatekeepers who set or block agendas behind the scenes. It may be wielded by internal or external agents over teachers and schools to influence what is taught or who is listened to in class, or it may be exercised through the informal structures of the school to exclude and discriminate against certain ideas and students. It may be wielded by NGOs with resources and influence to bypass formal decision makers and structures – in which case their power may be hidden or visible. Invisible power is a potent form of power which shapes the psychological and ideological boundaries of change (Miller et al. 2006: 12). It is power which shapes the 'taken for granted' and makes injustices like poverty seem 'natural' and racism, sexism and corruption invisible within the school. It is about stereotypes which are internalized such as the belief in certain societies that girls are intellectually inferior to boys or less able in maths and science (e.g. see Sanou and Aikman 2005; Stromquist 2007).

Henkel and Stirrat (2001) warn that there is much naivety about the complexities of power. And, of course, there is power embedded in participation itself. Meanings and practices of participation and decision-making need to be discussed and negotiated between development practitioners, young people, teachers and community. Enabling young people's access, presence and influence clearly means considering forms of power and the way they interact to provide barriers or opportunities for change, and to use this to develop strategies to enable young people's active participation.

Strategies for participation

The Mindanao programme developed in 2001 followed a strategy aimed at changing power dynamics to transform the school from an authoritarian and dysfunctional place to a democratic space where young people's voice could be nurtured. A preliminary evaluation of the Mindanao programme in 2003 showed higher levels of attendance and children's interest and participation in class. In contrast with earlier outbreaks of violence, the conflicts since 2003 have resulted in only brief interruptions in schooling as young people and their families are determined that schooling should continue (Angeles-Bautista 2003).

More recently the programme has developed a complementary set of strategies addressing different levels of the education system, for example linking financing issues at the local level to monitoring national budgets through the activities of the educational network, E-NET, and working for the adoption of the international Minimum Standards for Education in Emergencies in local and regional arenas. It works to ensure vertical linkages between local school contexts, decentralized and national levels of government and decision-making and policy-setting forums. As Gaventa (2006) highlights, key powerful actors are increasingly geographically distant from the local injustices they produce. For Oxfam, power analysis and local-to-global advocacy are the hallmark of its approach (Green 2008). It has also expanded activities horizontally from the school and teachers to train key players in the wider educational environment such local school boards and parent–teacher associations in providing support for internally displaced people and conflict resolution (Oxfam GB 2006).

This chapter has demonstrated the complexities of promoting children's active participation in poverty- and conflict-affected schools. But it has demonstrated the importance of children being active decision makers empowered to influence decisions in all aspects of educational development – from access to schooling and the culture of the school to influencing what is taught and how. It has examined ways in which power in and around the school can affect young people's ability to be decision makers. This indicates the importance for development programmes to map and analyse the dynamics of power in order to work towards democratic schools in chronic poverty and conflict contexts.

Angeles-Bautista (2003: 16) writes frankly about the Mindanao programme:

> Ironically, it was a crisis that made it possible ... if not for an emergency the convergence of partners would not have been necessary ... the pace of work would have been different; the teachers and supervisors would have been less receptive to 'intrusion'. But overwhelmed teachers sought support and were open to exploring alternative ideas and learning about better practices.

A key to long-term sustainable change will be through a range of interlinked strategies aimed at changing an authoritarian dysfunctional schooling system and building meaningful partnerships at many levels. As Gaventa (2006: 30) suggests, transformational change happens at rare moments when it is possible to work across dimensions of power effectively. The Mindanao programme saw a unique opportunity in the midst of conflict to work through the school for profound change. This long-term process of transformation continues with young people and their active participation at its heart.

Notes

[1] The discussion does not evaluate or analyse the project but uses it as a starting point for discussion. I wish to thank especially Alexandra Pura and Lan Mercado for their feedback and comments on this chapter and also Abraham Conneh and Maguy Mukidi for their stimulating discussion during the workshop in Manila in 2006. I was Oxfam GB Education Policy Adviser in 2001–7, but the views expressed in this chapter reflect my personal analysis.

[2] There is not space here to enter into details of differences between countries with 'fragile states' and those such as the Philippines where the conflict is regional, though these are significant factors. For further reading see International Save the Children Alliance (2006).

[3] The material for this section and all reference to the 'Mindanao programme' are taken from Oxfam GB (2002, 2005, 2006) and Angeles-Bautista (2003).

[4] Oxfam GB works in partnership with Community of Learners Foundation (COLF), BALAY Rehabilitation Centre and the Civil Society Network for Education Reforms E-NET.

References

Angeles-Bautista, F. de (2003) Creating schools that heal and teach peace. Unpublished manuscript.

Conneh, A. (2008) 'A hopeful future: men learning from women leaders in Liberia'. *Equals Newsletter*, 21 July: 7.

Davies, L., Williams, C. and Yamashita, H. with Ko Man-Hing, A. (2005) *Inspiring Schools: Impacts and Outcomes*. London: Centre for International Education and Research, Carnegie Young People Initiative.

Gaventa, J. (2006) 'Finding the spaces for change: a power analysis'. *IDS Bulletin*, 37(6), 23–33.

Goetz, A.M. and Gaventa, J. (2001) 'From consultation to influence: bringing citizen voice and client focus in to service delivery', IDS Working Paper 138. Brighton: Institute of Development Studies.

Green, D. (2008) *From Poverty to Power: How Active Citizens and Effective States Can Change The World*. Oxford: Oxfam,.

Henkel, H. and Stirrat, R. (2001) 'Participation as spiritual duty: empowerment as secular subjection', in B.Cooke and U. Kothari (eds), *Participation: The New Tyranny?* London: Zed, pp.168–84.

Inter-Agency Network for Education in Emergencies (2004) *Minimum Standards for Education in Emergencies, Chronic Crises and Early Reconstruction*. Paris: INEE.

International Save the Children Alliance (2006) *Rewrite the Future: Education for Children in Conflict-Affected Countries*. London: International Save the Children Alliance.

Kabeer, N. (2002) 'Citizenship and the boundaries of acknowledged community: identity, affiliation and exclusion', IDS *Working Paper171*. Brighton: Institute of Development Studies.

Miller, V., L. VeneKlasen, M. Reilly and C. Clarke. (2006) 'Making Change Happen: Power. Concepts for Revisioning Power for Justice, Equality and Peace', *Making Change Happen* 3. Washington, DC: Just Associates.

Oxfam GB (2002) 'Poverty in Central Mindanao'. Unpublished Oxfam/Ed Quitoriano, study, Manila, November.

Oxfam GB (2005) 'Oxfam programme and learning system'. Internal document PHLA89, Oxfam GB.

Oxfam GB (2006) 'Strengthening schools and community structures as focal points for community reconstruction and conflict resolution'. Unpublished programme proposal.

Sanou, S. and Aikman, S. (2005) 'Pastoralist schools in Mali: gendered roles and curriculum realities', in S. Aikman and E. Unterhalter (eds), *Beyond Access: Transforming Policy and Practice for Gender Equality in Education*. Oxford: Oxfam, pp. 181–98.

Smith, A. (2004) 'Education in the 21st century: conflict, reconstruction and reconciliation'. Plenary Address at the British Association for Comparative and International Education (BAICE) conference, Education in the 21st Century: Conflict, Reconstruction and Reconciliation, University of Sussex, 3–5 September.

Stromquist, N. (2007) 'The gender socialization process in schools: A cross-national comparison'. Background paper prepared for the *Education for All Global Monitoring Report 2008*, UNESCO.

Tawil, S and Harley, A. (eds) (2004) *Education, Conflict and Social Cohesion*. Geneva: International Bureau of Education.

Chapter 4

Long time coming: children as only occasional decision makers in schools

Clive Harber

Introduction

Schools run as near-dictatorships – as those most popular with parents sometimes are – cannot expect to produce critical active citizens without themselves being more democratic and listening to what their pupils have to say.

(Leader, *Times Educational Supplement*, 6 October 2006)

This chapter argues that, despite what we know from research about pupils' views of schooling and despite the evidence on the benefits of pupil involvement in decision-making, genuine pupil participation in decision-making in schools is still a comparatively rare phenomenon internationally.

School children as not decision makers

The daily reality of schooling for many, if not most, pupils globally is *not* one of participating in decision-making either about school organization or their own learning. This is despite most countries being signatories to the UN Convention on the Rights of the Child, and despite the argument that democracy is learned behaviour – in order to develop democratic values and behaviours we have to see and experience democratic practice. For example, in his detailed empirical five nation study of culture and pedagogy, Alexander (2000) was struck by the pervasive sense of control in all five schooling systems – America, England, France, India and Russia. The mechanisms, he argues, are universal – structure, curriculum, assessment, inspection, qualifications, school organization and teaching. The controlling function is exercised at different levels:

At national level (or state level in the United States) governments devise policies and structures, allocate budgets, determine goals, define curricula and institute mechanisms for assessing and policing what goes on at the system's lower levels. At regional and local levels such systems may be replicated or, depending on the balance of control over what goes on in the classrooms, they may simply be implemented. At school level, heads exercise varying degrees of influence or direct control over what goes on in classrooms; and at the end of the line, in classrooms, children are every day subjected to the pedagogic controls of teaching and curriculum. These controls extend into the furthest recesses of task, activity and interaction, and are mediated through routine, rule and ritual. Comparative macro-micro analysis illuminates the way these stack up and cumulatively impact on the child.

(Alexander 2000: 562)

Indeed, in *Schooling As Violence* (Harber 2004) I argued at some length and gathered together considerable documentary evidence to the effect that, while there are obviously exceptions, the dominant model of schooling globally is authoritarian, with pupils having very little say in what is learned, when, where or how. Although this authoritarianism is sometimes quite benign and benevolent, in other circumstances it creates a situation where children are bullied, beaten, sexually abused, physically and mentally harmed by stress and taught to hate other human beings and how to kill them. Having found it surprisingly easy to come across so much very disturbing evidence, the more interesting question for me is not why children truant or become rebellious and violent or why parents do not send their children to school, but the opposite – why do so many children still go to school and remain so pleasant and compliant? This perspective is supported by research on pupils' own views of schooling.

Pupil perspectives on schooling

Research on pupils' perspectives has existed in the UK since the late 1960s (Meighan and Siraj-Blatchford 2003: Ch. 2) and has covered a range of aspects of schooling, including how it can be used to enhance school effectiveness and improvement (Rudduck et al. 1996; Flutter and Rudduck 2004). The focus here is on more recent research issues relevant to pupils as decision makers. A survey of 15,000 British pupils carried out by the *Guardian* newspaper in 2001 on the topic of 'The School I'd Like' (later published in Burke and Grosvenor 2003) found that pupils felt that schools were not happy places, that pupils' views were not listened to, that they were not treated and respected as individuals and that schools were rigid and inflexible institutions.

A study of primary school children in Ireland found that 'in general children defined their relationships with their teachers in terms of control and regulation ... school was experienced as something that was done to them and over which they exercised little control' (Devine 2003: 138–40). In America a recent book on pupil perspectives on schooling was entitled *Fires in the Bathroom*. It was called this because:

> It's a safe bet that in random high schools across the United States, some kid has just set the bathroom wastebasket on fire. And deep down, all of us know why. Anyone who has made it out of their teens most likely remembers the feeling of anonymity and captivity that even the best high schools can convey.
>
> (Cushman, 2003: ix)

A recent study of children's views of schooling in Indonesia noted that this was one of the first of its kind because children's views on education are not usually taken into account by researchers or by teachers and educational policy makers:

> parents and policy makers at all levels make decisions and formulate policies generally on the basis of adults' perspectives. Their policies related to children's necessities are mostly focussed on the provision and the protection of the children based on adult views whereas children's right to participation is neglected and remains a formality.
>
> (Wibowo 2005: 190)

However, even though they have not traditionally been listened to, the study made clear the children had views that could be of benefit to those who make and implement educational policy.

Recent research on rural schooling in South Africa took into account the views of learners as well as parents and teachers (Nelson Mandela Foundation 2005). Despite significant democratic reform of educational policy since the end of apartheid, the situation on the ground in rural areas remains stubbornly authoritarian. Quotations from pupils provide a very clear picture of the realities of schooling in this context and strongly suggest that lessons are still mainly teacher-centred and that pupils are expected to be passive. According to the pupils, classroom activity is dominated by three modes: reading, writing and correcting. Corporal punishment is now illegal in South Africa, but it is evident from the pupils that it is still widespread. The pupils are clear that they do not like this and have many other views on how their schooling could be improved. One key point for many children in this context is that an important first step before more positive meaningful participation can take place is the removal of existing negative experiences.

For many of these children even a more benign form of authoritarianism would be a step forward. The report points to the 'unfreedoms within schools, which hinder the development of the capabilities for full human functioning in a democracy' (p. 81).

So, when researchers listen to pupils they tend to hear about an experience of schooling which does not on the whole involve pupils either as decision makers at school level or even as routine participants in their own learning. In some contexts schooling actually humiliates and hurts children. Even when young people do participate in school structures this is tokenistic because of their exclusion from the central purpose of schooling – teaching and learning. In the UK, for example, it is now estimated by Schools Council UK that around 90 per cent of secondary and 65–75 per cent of primary schools have school councils (Moggach 2006), though these vary greatly in their powers and responsibilities and, in the context of the national curriculum, it is debatable how many have any real influence on teaching and learning. Indeed, a recent study of pupil participation in primary schools in England using visual images as part of action research was notably tentative about what was possible: 'children and teachers felt constrained by invisible parameters about what they could or should discuss in meetings and by assumed hierarchical relationships. There was a tendency for school councils to deal with playground issues and fundraising, for example, rather than to discuss teaching and learning' (Cox et al. 2006: 11–12).

In the recent report on pupil participation in English secondary schools (Davies et al. 2006) what is striking is that in the case study schools pupils get to have a say on toilets, the canteen, food, lockers, fund-raising, the school newspaper and special events but, while these are important in terms of pupil motivation and self-esteem (and with the exception of some sixth-formers), very little on the curriculum itself unless it was how to deliver it better – for example, through peer tutoring, homework policy, information and communication technologies or classroom seating.

Children's voice: why is nobody listening?

There is now considerable international and comparative literature on democratic education which includes the many arguments supporting it (e.g. Apple and Beane 1995; Carnie 2003; Chapman et al. 1995; Davies and Kirkpatrick 2000; Harber 1998a, Harber 2004: Ch. 10; Harber and Davies,1997: Ch. 9; Schweisfurth et al. 2002; Trafford 2003). In this literature there is also evidence that listening to pupils, encouraging their participation and giving them more power and responsibility (i.e. greater democratization) can enhance school effectiveness and facilitate school improvement. First, in terms of conventional indicators of effectiveness:

- Rutter et al. (1979), in their major study of schools in the UK, found that schools that give a large proportion of students responsibility had better examination results, better behaviour and attendance and less delinquency.

- Harber (1993) found in interviews with Tanzanian teachers and pupils that they felt that greater pupil participation in decision-making improved communication in the school, reduced discipline problems and increased the confidence and discussion skills of learners. Lwehabura (1993) also studied four schools in Tanzania that faced financial problems, resource shortages and low teacher morale. He found that, both in the ability to deal with practical problems of stringency and in terms of examination success, the more democratically organized the school, the more effective (or perhaps less ineffective) it was. Similar, though more indicative, evidence exists on Ghana (Dadey and Harber 1991: 15–16).

- Trafford in his study in one British school in the mid-1990s, and Hannam (2001), in his study in the early 2000s of 12 schools manifestly describing themselves as 'student participative', found that there was a significant effect on both A-level and GCSE examination grades, in Hannam's case a judgement also supported by Ofsted (Trafford 2003: 15).

- There is also evidence from Britain that more participation in school decision-making, including school councils, can reduce levels of school exclusions (Hannam 2001; Commission for Racial Equality 1997; Davies 1998).

- In a review of the large literature on school effectiveness, Dimmock (1995) argues that there are some generally agreed findings accepted across cultures and systems and that these are linked to student participation. 'Classroom organisation which encourages and rewards student involvement is linked to higher learning. Achievement is higher where students take responsibility for their own learning ... Students in effective schools are treated with dignity and encouraged to participate in the organisation of the school ... The effective school culture includes many of the core values associated with democracy, such as tolerating and respecting others, participating and expressing views, sharing and disseminating knowledge, valuing equity and equality and the opportunity for students to make judgements and choices.'

- A longitudinal study of the graduates of democratically organized Sudbury Valley School in America found they had gone on to good colleges and good jobs because the school had created traits in them such as a strong sense of responsibility, the ability to take the initiative to solve problems, an ability to communicate effectively and a high commitment to the field in which employment is sought (Gray and Chanoff 1986).

- An empirical study of the practice of pupil democracy in Denmark, Holland, Sweden and Germany (Davies and Kirpatrick 2000: 82) concluded: 'It seemed to everyone clear that when pupils had a voice and were accorded value, the school was a happier place; where pupils are happy and given dignity, they attend more and they work more productively'.

- A recent study of pupil participation in seven English secondary schools (Davies et al. 2006) found that there was increased trust between teachers and pupils, behaviour improved and relationships improved between the school and the wider community.

- Finally, on a somewhat more speculative note, pupils in Finland participate actively in decision-making in schools at local, regional and national levels through a national school pupils' organization. Something must be working because Finland has come top of the international league tables in maths, mother tongue and science. Lord Adonis, the UK Schools Minister, recently visited Finland and reported back to the House of Commons education select committee that 'I was struck by the degree of pupil participation in the schools. School governing bodies now routinely in Finland have pupils as full members. That is something we don't have here' (Murphy 2006).

In terms of the contribution to democratic values:

- Research findings from America and Britain suggest that more democratic schools contributed to both participatory skills and the values of operating democratically (Hepburn 1984; John and Osborne 1992).

- There is evidence that more open, democratic classrooms making greater use of discussion and other participatory methods can foster a range of democratic political orientations such as greater political interest, greater political knowledge and a greater sense of political efficacy (Ehman 1980).

- Democratic and cooperative teaching methods have been shown to reduce inter-ethnic conflict and promote cross-cultural friendship (Lynch 1992:22).

- A study of five racially mixed schools in America compared two schools that stressed cooperative learning, interpersonal relationships, and clarification of values with three more traditional schools where students were streamed by achievement and lectured at in predominantly same-race classes. The study found that cross-race interaction and friendships and positive evaluation of students of different race were significantly higher in the more participative schools than in the more traditional, authoritarian ones (Conway and Damico 1993).

- A study of a desegregated school in South Africa that had also adopted a more democratic ethos and structures found that there was a dramatic decrease in racist comments and incidents in the schools as a result (Harber 1998b; Welgemoed 1998).

This literature cites many concrete and specific examples of successful democratic practice in education in both state and private and primary and secondary schools and in home-based education, though what learners have power over varies from context to context and case to case.

We know that it can and does work and can have considerable benefits for both pupils as schools as a whole, but also that globally it remains a minority sport. Why is this? To a certain extent the specific reasons vary from context to context. However, there also more fundamental problems with schooling.

Throughout the history of schooling there has always been a conflict between education for control in order to produce citizens and workers who were conformist, passive and politically docile on the one hand, and those who wanted to educate for critical consciousness, individual liberation and participatory democracy on the other. I have argued at length elsewhere (Harber 2004) that the former has dominated the real world of schooling, as opposed to educational debates and theory, because this was the main reason why formal, mass schooling systems were established in the first place and then expanded numerically and geographically through colonialism. Some educational writers, practitioners and policy makers have championed the latter approach to education, but the global persistence of the dominant authoritarian model suggests that the original purpose of control and compliance is deeply embedded in schooling and is highly resistant to change as a result.

Conclusion

For most children schooling does not presently provide much opportunity to participate in decision-making about significant school issues, especially in relation to curriculum, teaching and learning. However, there are researched and documented exceptions to this, and where they exist there have been benefits to both schools and pupils. This chapter has tried to explain why such approaches are not more common internationally and why there is still much to be done to increase the extent to which children really do act as decision makers in schools internationally.

References

Alexander, R. (2000) *Culture and Pedagogy: International Comparisons in Primary Education.* Oxford: Blackwell.

Apple, M. and Beane, J. (1999) *Democratic Schools: Lessons from the Chalk Face.* Buckingham: Open University Press.

Burke, C. and Grosvenor, I. (2003) *The School I'd Like: Children and Young People's Reflections on an Education for the 21st Century.* London: RoutledgeFalmer.

Carnie, F. (2003) *Alternative Approaches to Education*. London: RoutledgeFalmer.

Chapman, J., Froumin, I. and Aspin, D. (1995) *Creating and Managing The Democratic School*. London: Falmer.

Commission for Racial Equality (1997) *Exclusion from School and Racial Equality: A Good Practice Guide*. London: Commission for Racial Equality.

Conway, M. and Damico, S. (1993) 'Facing up to multiculturalism: Means as ends in democratic education'. Paper delivered to the International Conference on Education for Democracy in a Multicultural Society', Jerusalem, Israel.

Cox, S., Currie, D., Frederick, K., Jarvis, D., Lawes, S. Millner, E., Nudd, K., Robinson-Pant, A., Stubbs, I., Taylor, T. and White, D. (2006) *Children Decide: Power, Participation and Purpose in the Primary Classroom*. Norwich: University of East Anglia/CfBT.

Cushman, K. (2003) *Fires in the Bathroom*. New York: New Press.

Dadey, A. and Harber, C. (1991) *Training and Professional Support for Headship in Africa*. London: Commonwealth Secretariat.

Davies, L. (1998) *School Councils and Pupil Exclusions*. Birmingham: Centre for International Education and Research, University of Birmingham.

Davies, L. and Kirkpatrick, G. (2000) *The Euridem Project: A Review of Pupil Democracy in Europe*. London: Children's Rights Alliance for England.

Davies, L., Williams, C. and Yamashita, H. with Ko Man-Hing, A. (2006) *Inspiring Schools: Case Studies for Change*. London, Esmee Fairbairn and Carnegie UK.

Devine, D. (2003) *Children, Power and Schooling*. Stoke on Trent, Trentham Books.

Dimmock, C. (1995) 'Building democracy in the school setting: the principal's role', in J. Chapman, I. Froumin and D. Aspin (eds), *Creating and Managing the Democratic School*. London: Falmer.

Ehman, L. (1980) 'The American high school in the political socialisation process', *Review of Educational Research*, 50.

Flutter, J. and Rudduck, J. (2004) *How To Improve Your School: Giving Pupils a Voice*. London: Continuum.

Gray, P. and Chanoff, D. (1986) 'Democratic schooling: What happens to young people who have charge of their own education?', *American Journal of Education*, 94(2).

Hannam, D. (2001) *A Pilot Study to Evaluate the Impact of Student Participation Aspects of the Citizenship Order on Standards of Education in Secondary Education*. London: Community Service Volunteers.

Harber, C. (1993) 'Democratic management and school effectiveness in Africa: Learning from Tanzania'. *Compare*, 23(3), 289–300.

Harber, C. (ed.) (1998a) *Voices For Democracy*. Nottingham: Education Now.

Harber, C. (1998b) 'Desegregation, racial conflict and education for democracy in the new South Africa'. *International Review of Education*, 44(4), 569–82.

Harber, C. (2004) *Schooling As Violence*. London: RoutledgeFalmer.

Harber, C. and Davies, L. (1997) *School Management and Effectiveness in Developing Countries*. London: Cassell.

Hepburn, M. (1984) 'Democratic schooling: five perspectives from research', *International Journal of Political Education*, 6.

John, P. and Osborn, A. (1992) 'The influence of ethos on pupils' citizenship attitudes'. *Educational Review*, 44(2).

Lwehabura, J. (1993) 'School effectiveness in Tanzania'. Unpublished PhD, University of Birmingham.

Lynch, J. (1992) *Education for Citizenship in a Multicultural Society.* London: Cassell.

Meighan, R. and Siraj-Blatchford, I. (2003) *A Sociology of Educating* (4th edn). London: Continuum.

Moggach, T. (2006) 'Every voice matters'. *Times Educational Supplement*, 6 June.

Murphy, M. (2006) 'Every child has a view', *Education Guardian*, 28 November.

Nelson Mandela Foundation (2005) *Emerging Voices*. Cape Town: HSRC Press.

Rudduck, J., Chaplain, R. and Wallace, G. (eds) (1996) *School Improvement: What Can Pupils Tell Us?* London: David Fulton.

Rutter, M., Maughn, B., Mortimore, P. and Ouston, J. (1979) *Fifteen Thousand Hours: Secondary Schools and their Effects on Children*. London: Paul Chapman.

Schweisfurth, M., Davies, L. and Harber, C. (2002) (Eds.) *Learning Democracy and Citizenship: International Experiences*. Oxford: Symposium Books.

Trafford, B. (2003) *School Councils, School Democracy and School Improvement: Why, What, How?* Leicester: SHA Publications.

Welgemoed, A. (1998) 'Democratising a school in South Africa', in C. Harber (ed.), *Voices for Democracy: A North-South Dialogue on Education for Sustainable Democracy*. Nottingham: Education Now, in association with the British Council.

Wibowo, R. (2005) 'Do adults listen to children's voices?' Unpublished Ed.D thesis, University of Birmingham.

Part 2

Children's decision-making: its impact on life in schools and the community

This part of the book looks at how children and young people have engaged as change agents in schools and beyond, both within individual organizations and as members of social networks. Five case studies are presented, examining how children set about making a difference, with examples of work at different levels of operation (schools, school councils and non-governmental organization (NGO) contexts) and focus (from corporal punishment in schools to issues of international concern such as fairtrade). The impact of children's decision-making can be seen in terms of changes in policy and practice (at national and at local level in schools and communities), as well as the enhanced confidence and communication skills that children gained through participation. This latter aspect is perhaps key to how far and under what circumstances these project interventions can be sustained by young people – particularly at the point at which they challenge existing power relations with teachers in schools and adult decision-making structures in the community. What comes across strongly in Part 2 is that participation in decision-making is in itself a form of education valued highly by the young people involved. By contrast, teachers, parents and adult community members often view such informal learning as competing (in terms of time and energy) with formal schooling – yet later come to recognize the important contribution to young people's education, as well as to improving lives in their communities.

Children's clubs in Nepal have become an increasingly significant structure for enhancing children's participation in decisions both inside and outside school. Established originally by NGOs, such clubs are now mobilizing children to focus on their rights, including challenging the use of corporal punishment in schools and in the home. Teeka Bhattarai looks at how children have taken on responsibility for ensuring discipline in schools and the reactions of their teachers. The mobilization of children around such social issues raises political and cultural challenges to existing educational practices in schools and communities. Although tackling corporal punishment can help to reduce school drop-out rates, teachers and parents were concerned that children had less time to study because they were involved in organizing such campaigns and that challenging 'the moral authority' of the teacher in this way could intensify political upheaval on a larger scale in society at large.

In Zambia, the NGO People's Action Forum has initiated a process involving the community in working to improve school effectiveness through participatory school governance. The policy context creates space for the participation of children, but, as Gina M. Chiwela describes, it is the intensive community-based sensitization work of the NGO that helps to change community and school attitudes to participation and to the potential of children, although how this is defined and enacted varies. This chapter gives an insight into how non-formal adult education can help to ensure that central policy designed to promote children's involvement in decision-making is actually translated into practice in communities.

Trippett, Bañez-Ockelford, Mamaliga, Saksena and Vigil analyse the impact of three projects supported by the NGO EveryChild in Peru, Moldova and India. Aimed at facilitating children's participation in decision-making within their communities, these projects were initially set up and supported by adults. They differed in how far they were focused on influencing a specific policy area (in the case of the conference on childcare reform in Moldova) or were intended to provide a new space for children's voices to be heard on a wide range of issues (the children's parliaments in Tamil Nadu and a child-run radio programme in Santa Maria de Chicmo). In all three cases, the young people brought a new perspective to previously adult-dominated policy agendas. They also demonstrated changes in their own lives in terms of enhanced confidence and communication skills gained through the process of participating in a decision-making forum, conference or radio programme. This chapter raises issues about 'scaling up' such activities: inevitably this leads to children having to engage more fully with adult decision-making structures rather than having the scope to change practices. In contrast to the UK contexts described in this part of the book, the lack of child protection concerns meant that the children in Peru, India and Moldova had greater opportunities for participating in decision-making and action, yet could also be regarded as exposed to more risks.

A fairtrade campaign initiated by the Development Education Centre in Liverpool (UK) provided the opportunity for young people to act as advocates and change agents in their home and school communities. Working directly with school councillors, rather than through teachers, the Liverpool

World Centre facilitators aimed to create a new space for young people to make decisions that would affect their communities. Like the EveryChild experiences, the young people described here gained in confidence once they were able to take the lead in educating their parents and teachers about fairtrade. Anne-Marie Smith gives an insight into the challenges faced in transforming adult attitudes and the cultures that constrained children's participation in decision-making, particularly in schools. The introduction of a 'new issue' like fairtrade to the school councils (rather than the more common issues around toilets and fund-raising), however, provided the opportunity for children to take the lead in making changes that influenced the lives of adults as well as young people.

Fiona Carnie discusses a project in Portsmouth (UK) that involved students in decision-making about their life in schools. Rather than being focused on one school, this collaborative project aimed to work across all the city schools. Students were encouraged to have more voice in the running of their schools, contributing to decisions about teaching and learning in their schools (such as how to organize homework) as well as to improving peer support to tackle problems like bullying. This case illustrates the benefits to teachers and students of sharing experiences between schools and the importance of integrating these approaches throughout a school, rather than assuming that the school council can work in isolation. However, long-term sustainability of these strategies requires significant changes in school cultures, as also illustrated by Chapters 8 and 15 in this book.

Chapter 5

Children's clubs and corporal punishment: reflections from Nepal

Teeka Bhattarai

The broader context

Sandwiched between the two largest Asian giants – China in the north and India in the south – Nepal is a land of cultural and ecological diversity. Whilst the Hindu belief system has influenced the governing of state and societal affairs, including education, many people practise Buddhism. Ranked amongst the least developed countries of the world, health and education facilities are very limited: still about a fifth of Nepal's children do not go to school at all since they have an economic role to play – looking after cattle, taking care of younger siblings and working in menial jobs such as carpet weaving. Punishment in school also contributes to school drop-out. Nepal borrowed an education system from colonial Britain through neighbouring India's influence – and from the point of view of corporal punishment, it remains more or less the same as in colonial times.

Corporal punishment in Nepal

Corporal punishment of various kinds (see Table 5.1) and for various reasons (see Table 5.2) is one of the significant causes of school drop-out in countries such as Nepal: a study in South Asia found that over 15% of children were scared of their teachers (Haq and Haq 1998), and in many cases this fear stops them attending school. Today corporal punishment still persists in Nepal, although it was made illegal in 2005 and is more prevalent in private than in government schools. The former compete strongly to produce good exam results so that they can attract more children (Lama 2006; Paudyal 2003), and, since the exams are based on memorizing and reproducing facts, rather than application and analysis, the threat of violence works well. As the parents also see a good return for their investment in terms of exam results, most do not mind punishment in school – many even demand it.

In conversation with teachers and parents in Nepal, it became evident to me that a level of fear was felt necessary for children to learn (see CVICT/UNICEF 2003; Rajbhandary et al. 1999). This also comes from the culture of giving secondary importance to children. In Hindu scriptures, children are projected as 'trouble' for securing your place in heaven, as they distract you from performing rituals or meditation and from devotion to god. A traditional moral code, Chanakya Neeti (dating back to the third century BC), clearly prescribed that 'children should be cuddled for the first five years, beaten for the next ten years and they should be treated as friends when they reach sixteen' (Chanakya n.d.).[1]

The European education system had a similarly negative influence: perhaps this comes from the practice of treating children as 'minors'. Nepal's Penal Code (1853), promulgated by Jang Bahadur Rana under the influence

Table 5.1 Types of punishment in vogue in schools

Physical punishments	Mental torture	Mixed punishments
• Caning • Wedging a pencil between their fingers • Locking child in the toilet (smelly toilets!) • Pulling hair from the temple • Pinching/twisting ears • Hitting with nettle plant • Acting as a hen/cock • Making them crawl like a toddler	• Scolding, using derogative terms • Making student stand naked • Isolating them in the classroom	• Making student stand on bench on one foot • Sit and stand in the classroom • Expulsion from the classroom • Asking a classmate to spank or cane or hit them

Source: Lama (2006)

Table 5.2 Common reasons for punishment

- Not submitting homework on time
- Making noise in the classroom
- Being absent or late
- Not wearing the proper uniform
- Vandalizing school property
- Breaching other school discipline, e.g. speaking mother tongue
- Not paying fees on time

of his visit to Britain, abolished many forms of physical mutilations but not corporal punishment (Andrea 1991).[2] Nepal waited until 2005 for corporal punishment to be outlawed, a consequence of ratifying the United Nations Convention on the Rights of the Child in 1993. From legal reform, however, it is a long way to realizing such a change. This chapter seeks to give an account of how children's clubs are working to enforce anti-corporal punishment laws in the country.

Children's clubs in Nepal

The context

Influenced by the rights-based approach to development, children's clubs have been established by many development organizations in Nepal. In the late 1980s, these clubs were being established to address environmental issues through establishing plantations and receiving education on conservation. Specific groups, such as mothers and youth, had already been working around development issues and so it was a natural move to mobilize children separately. The origin of the idea appears to be a radio programme with UNICEF support back in 1982 when a fictional children's club was used in radio drama conversations (Rajbhandary et al. 1999). The spread of children's clubs coincided with the mushrooming growth of non-governmental organizations (NGOs) after the People's Movement of 1990. Institutions with a specific remit for children (such as Save the Children) have taken the clubs further through promoting the issue of child rights and giving financial support. Already before the turn of the millennium, some 300 children's clubs were working in project areas of Save the Children Norway and Save the Children US (Rajbhandary et al. 1999), and it is estimated that they now exist in their thousands. In terms of spread, the number of children's clubs appears to be higher in the areas where many development agencies are working. Active children's club members often come from families where adults are also involved in community activities, although in some cases 'development enters' through the children.

The most active members of the clubs are from the early teenage years. Normally they are not considered to be children after they leave school, though this idea is changing due to international influences. Although the clubs are not formed around a particular school, leadership of the clubs is most often found to have rested on the academically good students of the school(s) of the area. Normally membership is open to all children in their 'command area'. The clubs generally have a seven- to eleven-member executive committee, diverse in terms of gender, ethnicity, geography, and age. There is a chair, treasurer and secretary who have more power and say than executive members. The chair is the most powerful – leading and maintaining public relations. Meeting normally once a month, the children's clubs are said to be more democratic than the organizations belonging to adults.

Corporal punishment as part of the clubs' remit

In general, children's clubs are felt to follow their immediate seniors, the youth clubs. These clubs, engaging largely in sports and cultural activities, were encouraged by the past regime to keep them away from politics. However, children's clubs – perhaps being the products of development actors and supported by NGOs – are more engaged in community activities, such as the cleaning of the village. Although most children's clubs now have protection of children's rights as their objective, it is felt to be abstract and yet to be translated into action. Preventing violence against children is increasingly coming into the list of their activities but because most children's clubs need support from adults and their elders still feel the need for some kind of punishment, such issues have not tended to be at the top of their priorities. In fact, in a recent survey, parents did not even mention the rights of children as a benefit of children's clubs. Rajbhandary et al. (1999) list the following activities of children's clubs in order of the intensity of their involvement:

- Artistic/cultural expression
- National rallies (e.g. children's day)
- Development work
- Play/recreation/sports
- Competitions (essays, quiz contest etc)
- Club management
- Skill development
- Promotion of community awareness.

The next section discusses two children's clubs that decided to work against corporal punishment.

The two cases

Everest Children's Club, Thimi, Bhaktapur

Located in Pobun, Thimi, Everest Children's Club was established in the year 2000. Currently, 40 children are members of the club,[3] though it had as many as 56 at one time. An 11-member executive committee, with a chair, vice chair, treasurer, secretary and seven executive members, holds meetings once a month. The drive to establish the club came through a local person who worked for UNICEF's Community Based Rehabilitation program in Bhaktapur, a nearby town. He also solicited some financial support and the children were provided with 15 days of intensive training. This was one of the first groups in their community and the club inspired adults to establish mothers' and fathers' groups, as well as savings and credit groups.

The thrust of their work is the overall development of children – through activities such as quiz contests, essay competitions, public speaking and special tuition for needy children. Cleaning streets is one of their regular activities. The club also conducted a survey to find out who was not going to school and why not, and managed to bring some students back to school by approaching parents and children. As tackling children's rights was one of their major objectives, the club provided training to children's groups in schools and discussed with teachers why it was important not to hit children. Teachers resisted at the beginning, but slowly accepted their ideas when the club approached them as a group.

All the executive members give credit to the club activities, particularly training, for gaining exposure to the outside world. The vice chairperson, Radhika Rajbahak (17), commented: 'Oh, impact? I wouldn't be able to speak to you like this if I was not in the club!' A former member noted changes that had taken place: 'When we behave well and pay attention in our studies, there is no need for punishment – this is what has happened.' Parents appear supportive and are now talking about the reactivation of the club, as it had lapsed for the past year. They pointed to two reasons: active members had grown older (and the next generation has not received adequate training) and had less time due to higher studies. They also lacked a space for meetings.

Naram Bal Bikas Children's Club, Nawalparasi

The idea of forming this club came from a community development project funded by ActionAid.[4] The club's area covers the area of one village development committee, with a population of a few thousand: a boy and girl attend from each of the nine wards. Children are automatically members from the age when they can speak until age 18. Some members have to walk for more than an hour in order to attend meetings.

The club lists the following major activities:

- 'Every child of school age' goes to school campaign
- Promoting children's rights
- Cleaning school/ village campaigns

- Regular meeting (monthly)
- Children's savings
- Wall newspaper publication.

The club's campaign of action against violence against children (including corporal punishment) means that any case of violence referred by someone is discussed in a meeting. They speak to parents and teachers (including counselling for affected children) when a child is subjected to violence. In the case of school, teachers now refer breaches of discipline to the club and they discuss how to handle them. At best, they try not to give any punishment for the first offence. Even in cases of serious misbehaviour (e.g. beating another child or vandalizing school property), they 'order' corrective measures such as cleaning the classroom or the playground. In the case of parents who 'do not listen to their advice', the story of the violence is published on the wall newspaper they publish fortnightly. They sometimes have to face angry parents for making the case public, but the club says it works as a mechanism for controlling violence in the household. Perhaps this also creates fear among teachers, though the club has faced fewer instances in schools where there is a general feeling that children are better disciplined due to the club's activities. Teachers say that there is no need to punish them when they are self-disciplined. There was also evidence that academic activity in school had improved.

Mediated by an external NGO in the beginning, the children have enjoyed full support from their parents, who encourage club membership and participation. Of course the club has its ups and downs, but its role in community leadership is key for them.

Impact of children's clubs

Although there has not been a systematic study on the clubs' impact on corporal punishment in schools, teachers say that children have become more responsible and the need for disciplinary action does not arise. One of the major impacts felt amongst children is that they speak out and their level of confidence is higher. This alone must have influenced how teachers respond to their students. The chair of Naram Children's Club said that teachers do not give them harsh punishment as they might 'lose face'. Children are often forgiven on the condition that they do not repeate the offence. The club members also follow them up in support of this. Members of the executive committee are expected to be self-disciplined and so far they have not committed a 'punishable' act.

Nonetheless, there is a feeling amongst some community members and teachers that after all it is the 'project people' who are behind the 'show'. Teachers obviously do not like it when a little girl challenges the punishment for a minor act (such as stamping on a bench with muddy shoes). Children have sometimes published information about unnecessary violence committed by certain parents, which has angered the individuals concerned, and the club has had to work hard to make a positive environment in the family for the child. Many adults feel that the club activities have prevented children from playing pranks and that they have learned new ideas, including how to run an institution. In general, children are reported to be democratic and inclusive, though whether they have always been objective in decision-making needs to be carefully scrutinized.

Pros and cons: a debate

With the formation of children's clubs, both children and teachers have seen positive changes. Firstly, the number of cases requiring disciplinary action has reduced dramatically. When teachers encounter misbehaving students, they now refer them to the club. When teachers are involved in actions that are against the rights of children, the club holds a dialogue with them and a compromise is sought. As discussed earlier, many children did not come to school for fear of punishment after they make a childish mistake. In such cases, these children clubs have been effective in counselling the child and asking for an 'amnesty' from the teacher. In the situation when even their own parents demand punishment for any wrongdoing, the child may have nobody to confide in. This peer-to-peer communication has proved very effective.

Some say children clubs are no different from the 'old system of having a class monitor' who ruled the class on behalf of the teacher. The monitor was often a child from the local elite and abused their authority. In areas where the 'monitor system' was in place, mostly it is now the same individuals who comprise the children's club. Some fear that when the school is at a higher level, the clubs function like trade unions and the moral authority of teacher has no meaning. In countries like Nepal, student unions in tertiary education have functioned as an extension of political parties, making undue demands and challenging the authority of teaching staff rather than concentrating on pertinent educational issues.

Another school of thought is that this is too much to expect from children. This is an extra burden for them: they should be studying at this age rather than bothering with such issues. Children's clubs take time and it is even less appropriate for poor children who also have to contribute to the family's livelihood. The need for the protection of children's rights should be the responsibility of teachers. People of this school of thought believe that because such children's clubs are the products of aid agencies, teachers simply have not been saying no to their activities: when external support comes to an end, they will be as oblivious to children's rights as before. Children's clubs, in their view, should just be confined to easier jobs to give them experience of practising self-organization.[5] So far, initiatives for children's clubs have not come from within the education sector so have no legitimacy within the system – teachers would not be obliged to conform to the decisions made by children's clubs, were it not for social pressure and influence of the donor agency concerned.

In the two cases here, corporal punishment was significantly reduced due to children's persuasive efforts. However, we need to promote more debate around some of the issues raised in this chapter: whether the clubs' role means that teachers sneak away from their responsibilities and give an undue burden to children in handling such a socially and practically complex issue as corporal punishment. When teachers are compelled to 'give up' punishment as a method of teaching, alternative methods are necessary – raising questions around pedagogy and teacher training. Once the children are used to having education mediated by children's clubs, their absence can create a vacuum to fill for both the teachers and the children. There is no assurance of the continuation of these clubs in the long run.

The existence of children's clubs is confined to a particular layer of Nepali society. The violence occurring in most private schools in the name of 'quality education' appears to be continuing unabated. Most children's clubs are focused on government schools that are increasingly left for the children of the poor and powerless sections of society. In this context, it is a real challenge for these clubs not to appear to parents as an unnecessary hindrance to children achieving a better education, not just in relation to exam results, but also to improving the quality of their lives. As an alternative strategy, teachers are being trained specifically on the rights of children and on the adoption of non-violent methods of teaching. The outcome of these two approaches (working with teachers and promoting children's clubs) needs now to be compared with regard to 'the burden' children have to take up in running children's clubs – particularly in dealing with the issue of corporal punishment in schools.

Notes

[1]   A scholar and politician whose work is known as a '(social) policy or code'.
[2]   Caning was banned in Britain as late as the end of the 1980s.
[3]   Pobun is a Newar community and all its members come from the same ethnic group.
[4]   A large international charity founded in Britain.
[5]   This relates to the issues raised in other chapters too about citizenship education: whether the aim is for children to make 'real' decisions that affect their lives now or to 'practise' decision-making in order to become more active citizens in the future (see Chapters 10 and 15).

References

Andrea, M. (ed.) (1991) *Jang Bahadur in Nepal: A Country Study,* Washington, DC: GPO for the Library of Congress

Chanakya, A. (n.d.) *Chanakya Neeti* [Chanakya's Code]. Original in Sanskrit with Nepali translations. Varanasi, India: Thimurti Prakashan.

CVICT/UNICEF (2003) *Discipline with Dignity*. Kathmanudu: Centre for the Victims of the Torture and UNICEF Nepal.

Haq, M. and Haq, K. (1998) *Human Development in South Asia*. Dhaka: University Press

Lama, S. (2006) 'Bidyalayamahune himsabirodhi abhiyan' [Campaign against corporal punishment in schools]. *Janamukhi Shiksha*, 7(16).

Paudyal, R. (2003) 'Corporal punishment in private school'. *The Rising Nepal*, 10 February.

Rajbhandary, J., Hart, R. and Khatiwada, C. (1999) *The Children's Clubs of Nepal: A Democratic Experiment, Summary and Recommendations from a Study of Children's Clubs*. Kathmandu: Save the Children (Norway and US).

Chapter 6

Participatory school governance: children in decision-making in the Zambian context

Gina Mumba Chiwela

Figure 6.1 1st grade learners in Nakasaka Community School – PAF Mumbwa, Zambia. (Courtesy: Gina Chiwela, Peoples Action Forum, 2009).

Introduction

People's Action Forum (PAF) is an indigenous Zambian non-profit non-governmental organization (NGO), most of whose membership is from the rural communities where PAF carries out its activities. Working with whole communities, especially with women and children, PAF's approach is to help local groups realize that their development cannot be some abstract body's responsibility, but must be their own; that rather than wait for government to decide what they need, people should insist on being involved in the decision-making processes to address issues concerning their communities' welfare.

PAF works in six strategic areas: capacity building; community initiatives; advocacy; communication, information and networking; resource mobilization: and HIV/AIDS. Within community initiatives, PAF utilizes the Reflect approach, a participatory methodology for critical analysis of issues and for social change. It is through these processes that target groups have identified the major needs for which they seek solutions: the primary concern being their children's education. To address these concerns, PAF interacts with other NGOs, both local and international, as well as with civil society organizations and government, especially those working in relation to education policy. The school governance programme discussed in this chapter is targeted at government, private and community schools.

PAF is a member of **PAMOJA** Africa Reflect Network,[1] which has developed an approach to enhance participation of whole communities in school governance. The Reflect non-formal education approach aims to create a space where people feel comfortable to meet and discuss issues relevant to their development. By using Reflect in school governance, parents can begin to analyse their school environment, identify school problems, come up with practical solutions and take positive action, gaining a sense of ownership of events and activities in the school (see Nandago et al. 2005). The aim of participatory school governance is to transform power relations, creating an open or democratic environment in which the voices of parents, school authorities and children are given equal weight.

This chapter reflects on PAF's non-formal education project, focusing on the benefits of participatory school governance, and on how children's voices and decisions have been incorporated in the process. Based on three case study schools from the participatory school governance programme, it extracts lessons which may be of relevance in other contexts.

Project background

The overall goal of the project is to enhance the quality of education through good school governance in which members of target communities are confident, fully engaged and involved. Resources provided to schools and other institutions often go to waste due to lack of accountability by those placed in charge. Those who are deemed to be outside the school system are not expected to inquire into utilization of public resources; neither do target groups know that they have the right to query office bearers. Hence there is a need to provide people with awareness of the nature of participation in public issues and with the skills to carry out such investigations. Participatory school governance is a process that allows communities to be part of the planning and management of schools, of which an integral part is raising funds, budgeting and tracing of resources from source to expenditure, or 'budget tracking'.

Through non-formal education, communities previously excluded from formal schooling have been able to acquire life skills relevant to their development. Research shows that many people are relapsing into illiteracy due to the limited initiatives that promote community education in Zambia (Machila 2005). Participatory school governance is one such vehicle for education that can enhance participation of whole communities in development and thereby contribute to reducing children's drop-out and illiteracy.

Why participatory school governance? And how is this relevant for children?

The scarcity of management information available to stakeholders in terms of processes, structures, institutional mechanisms, functions and opportunities for participation undermines their capacity to engage effectively in planning, budgeting and management of schools. Additionally, the exceptional centralization of decision-making in education greatly limits the degree to which parents, local communities, teachers, civic leaders, district education authorities, civil society groups, and children can influence management and decision-making processes and make legitimate demands to improve the quality of education.

Against this background, it is vital to identify ways in which stakeholders can effectively be facilitated to participate. In this scenario it is easy to overlook children and their specific social position, even when named as stakeholders. In working in participatory school governance, PAF has found that children also have something to say about their schools and how they should be run. PAF found that participation in school governance and stakeholders' expectations varied across different communities – from seeing the child as doing their part by simply making sure they go to school, to declaring that children do have a significant part to play in decision-making. The insight gained from community discussions and school visits has led to interest in how the child as a primary stakeholder in education and the life of a school can be helped to participate in decision-making.

An adult's capacity and confidence to engage in decision-making is often predicated on the ability to communicate effectively. The inability to read and write, as one means of communication, may limit participation in the necessary investigative and management processes. Sometimes illiterate people feel that they are unable to stand shoulder-to-shoulder with fellow parents who are literate or with school authorities – even if they have some relevant knowledge that others may not have. Most women are the first educators of their children, but despite this central role they are sometimes sidelined in development (Open Society Initiative for South Africa 2008). The programme of participation offers women continuity in this role in the school environment.

Structures of school governance

Basic education in Zambia falls under the jurisdiction of the district education board. At the school level the school manager (headteacher) and teachers are the primary decision makers in school matters. The parent–teacher association (PTA) represents the parental and community input into the running of the school. The school manager is the secretary, while teachers sit on the committees to represent the school. The PTA consists of several different committees that look into specific areas of school management such as finances, fund-raising and disciplinary matters. In its governance the school also works through a prefecture headed by a head boy and head girl who have several prefects under their supervision. Their role is to maintain discipline and order, and to ensure that decisions that directly affect pupils are carried out.

Policies on participation

The Zambian Ministry of Education is guided by the national policy that states that: 'Guided by the principle that communities have a basic right to provide education at all levels, the Ministry will encourage and facilitate full participation of communities in educational provision' (Ministry of Education 1996).

In its seven strategies to achieve full community participation, the 'community' referred to here is that of adults. Children are recognized as the direct beneficiaries of this participation, but their role in school governance is not defined. At a lower level this is reflected in the PTA guidelines in the Education Act where children are not reflected at all as stakeholders with decision-making rights in basic schools. Parallel to this, high school boards have clearly defined guidelines for the participation of children. In 2006, Zambia revised its National Child Policy, which provides guidance on all matters related to child welfare. The multi-sectoral approach to interventions ultimately impacts on specific areas of child participation in the school through areas such as child health, HIV/AIDS, and environment. Children with disabilities, and orphaned and vulnerable children are also considered in the policy (Ministry of Sport, Youth and Child Development 2006). Specific policy issues affecting school governance include:

- Free basic education. Grade 1–9 education is free. The national policy states that: 'The provision and funding of early childhood and preschool education will be the responsibility of Councils (local Government), local communities, non-governmental organisations, private individuals and families' (Ministry of Education 1996: 22). Furthermore: 'Local communities will participate in the development, maintenance and repair of basic schools.' (Ministry of Education 1996: 8). Parents have been led to believe they have no part in contributing to school improvement by the words 'free education'.
- Decentralization policy. 'The Ministry will negotiate with local authorities, church groups and other bodies for the resumption by these bodies of some of the responsibility they had in the past for the management of schools.' (Ministry of Education 1996: 22). The policy is intended to devolve responsibility for school management to local government, which, like the communities, currently has no capacity to effectively run educational institutions.
- Re-entry policy. Following this policy, pregnant girls are permitted to remain in school during pregnancy and encouraged to return after giving birth. It addresses a critical situation that rates among the top three reasons why children leave school (Ward and Gwaba 2006). Teachers are finding relationships with these girls strained, making them reluctant to allow children the space to freely give their opinion. It was found that the policy has been applied without pupils being helped to understand their role and responsibility in successful implementation. Those that fall 'victim' to this situation often seem not to appreciate why they are back in school, while fellow pupils often do not readily accept them back.

Decision-making practices in schools

The participation policies in educational provision and school improvement give space for encouraging and enhancing greater participation of children in decision-making for school governance. However, the struggle around handing over decision-making to children, along with the fear of 'anarchy' should this be allowed, is a common challenge in schools in Zambia, as elsewhere. In the UK schools described in this volume (see Chapters 8 and 15), teachers felt that as professionals, they 'were obliged to take ultimate responsibility for decisions' (Cox et al. 2006). These common attitudes towards children's participation help to illuminate the gap between policy and practice in Zambian schools.

This gap was identified and confirmed in a project supported by the Commonwealth Education Fund in education budget tracking and analysis in Zambia. Nine partner organizations were involved in training communities, teachers in community schools and members of staff and volunteers of civil society organizations in budget analysis and tracking and also conducting the actual tracking in selected schools. As one of the partners experienced in participatory approaches to adult learning, PAF proposed broadening the work in participatory school governance to go beyond mere involvement in tracking of funds in the education system. PAF therefore conducted training of 20 local and international partners.[2]

The participatory school governance programme involved visits for training in participatory school governance, community sensitization and monitoring visits to government schools, community schools (initiated and run largely by communities) and private schools. In total, 26 schools (12 government (basic schools), 8 community and 2 private schools) were visited by the nine partners between May and October 2006. Fifteen of these were from the PAF work in three districts where at each school the school manager, deputy, bursar, PTA chairperson, finance committee member and/ or other committee members were in attendance. From their discussions, the following points on the situation prevalent in the schools emerged:

- What may be understood and applauded as child participation is at its best actively involving them in implementing decisions made by adults. This was found, for example, at Nyau Basic School where pupils expressed ignorance at being represented on the planning committee or PTA. The adults emphatically pointed out that they had children's full participation. On further inquiry, this was actually found to mean that once parents and teachers had made decisions, the children took part in implementation, for example ferrying sand to the building site. They were not required to say what they thought about the necessity and use of a new building, nor how they would participate.
- Twelve out of the 15 schools reported a good working relationship, with the parents taking a lead in school improvement.
- In three of the schools the PTAs were merely asked to approve and implement plans made by the school manager and teachers.
- Children are represented on the different school committees. They are expected to report to the prefecture and ensure decisions taken are carried out. Some were emphatic that children's opinions and suggestions are given consideration, a claim authenticated by the pupils in some but denied in other schools.

Attitudes at community level

New school improvement programmes introduced in schools by the Ministry of Education and donors have required the involvement of children. This has led to child participation being 'taken on board' in many cases without appreciation of the real levels of participation required to make a difference. The range of opinion expressed in the school and by community members was wide. Some were supportive, commenting:

> Children are very much a part of decision-making. They are the ones learning here and know what they want the school to be like.

> Children also have ideas that adults can learn from.

> They sit in on our Committee meetings so they can report back to their friends.

> [As teachers] we see that these children are able to talk in class and express their views, it means they have something to contribute to the governance of the school.

Others were not quite as accepting or found the concept a little difficult. One teacher said:

> It is difficult to involve children, they would make noise in the meetings.

A parent member of the PTA said:

> They participate by being present in school. That's all they should do. They are not even asked to help in the physical work projects.

Another parent in the community expressed the view that:

> Children cannot understand anything; it is our job as adults and parents to plan for them and provide what they need ... But how can we involve children?

The children interviewed were found to be willing to participate, and confident that they had something to say about the running and welfare of the schools. They were not aware that schools receive a grant from the Ministry of Education for running costs of the school. They had comments on many issues:

> They only use the money for chalk and sports days out, we don't know what they do with the rest of the PTA funds.

We know what we want. If they had asked us we would have told them to build a school hall rather than a classroom block.

How can a teacher perform well in class when he has no place to sleep? They should build teachers houses.

The other school looks better than ours because everybody there works together.

They can ask us also what we think because many of us have parents or grandparents who haven't been to school and don't know what they should do to help us.

These were the comments from randomly selected children from the schools visited, indicating that they have an opinion about how their school environment affects them and how it should be improved.

Obstacles to children's participation

There are a number of barriers to the effective involvement of children in decision-making concerning their education. Among the most significant in this study were the following:

- The cultural attitude – children are brought up to believe they should remain silent in the presence of adults. Hence the child may be hesitant to speak, while the adult is uncomfortable with the child who expresses an opinion.
- A lack of knowledge of how exactly this participation can be brought about, and lack of exposure to a model that has worked.
- Political influence that wishes to win support for the provision of free education and keeps parents comfortable in leaving everything to school authorities.
- Ignorance and illiteracy were emphasized in both schools and communities as a major cause for the low confidence and capacity of the parents to participate in school governance.

The case studies referred to above focused on three basic schools (primary schools extended to run beyond Grades 1–7 to Grade 9), the decision-making structures and policies in which they operate, and practice found on the ground, in the context of the training and sensitization taking place. The different findings from the three schools served to illustrate both the potential enthusiasm for participation, and the barriers, both structural and attitudinal, as discussed above.

Conclusion and lessons for the future

The partnership policy allows for innovation in how communities can participate in school governance, making space for children to be involved in decision-making. Advocacy for clearer definition of the roles of children needs to emphasize their places as key stakeholders in education and will give direction to communities in how to make participation happen. A clear policy direction could encourage schools and give them a mandate to actively develop the participation of pupils. Clearer guidelines would also delineate structures in a way that any conflict or ambiguity would be avoided to remove apprehension and suspicions in partnering efforts.

In its contribution to this goal, PAF sees its place as increasing adult participation through changing attitudes in schools and communities by means of ongoing awareness raising. PAF strongly supports the child's right to develop as stated in the UN Convention on the Rights of the Child, ratified by Zambia in 1991. Additionally, non-formal education through ongoing Reflect programmes can develop people's capacity to engage in school affairs. PAF helps change schools' attitudes in order to become welcoming, open and transparent in their cooperation with communities. PAF also aims to build children's capacity to participate by enhancing physical and mental health through school nutrition programmes and psychosocial counselling training for teachers. Children's analytical and negotiating skills can be enhanced through the use of the Reflect process.

Truly participatory school governance practice is a long process because it involves a major changes in attitudes. Communities must be liberated to 'walk into the school yard' with all confidence, knowing that this is their place of responsibility and will be part of a better future for their children and community as a whole. The participation of children in decision-making is a critical and indispensable part of this process.

Notes

[1] The Commonwealth Education Fund supported the initial development of the approach and training manual by PAMOJA Africa Reflect Network. The Fund facilitated PAF's work with local communities and schools and the training of ten local NGOs in participatory school governance.

[2] These partners shared and documented their experiences and lessons learnt at the end of the project (see Commonwealth Education Fund Zambia 2008).

References

Commonwealth Education Fund Zambia (2008) *Civil Society Education Budget Analysis and Tracking: A Report Documenting Commonwealth Education Fund Budget Analysis and Tracking Experiences in Zambia.* Lusaka: Oxfam.

Cox, S., Currie, D., Frederick, K., Jarvis, D., Lawes, S., Millner, E., Nudd, K. Robinson-Pant, A., Stubbs, I., Taylor, T. and White, D. (2006) 'Children Decide: Power, Participation & Purpose in the Primary Classroom'. Norwich: University of East Anglia

Machila, M. (2005) *People's Action Forum. Strategic Plan 2005–2007.* Lusaka

Ministry of Education (1996) *Educating our Future: National Policy on Education.* Lusaka: ZEPH.

Ministry of Sport, Youth and Child Development (2006) *National Child Policy 2006.* Lusaka: MSYCD.

Nandago, M., Obondoh, A. and Otiende, E. (2005) *Managing Our Schools Today. A Practical Guide to Participatory School Governance.* Kampala: Real Press.

Open Society Initiative for Southern Africa (2008) *Adult Literacy: Putting Southern African Policy and Practice into Perspective.* Johannesburg: OSISA.

Ward, P. and Gwaba, R.M. (2006) *Children's Rights in Zambia: A Situation Analysis.* Pretoria: Save The Children Sweden.

Chapter 7

EveryChild: NGO experiences with children as decision makers in Peru, India and Moldova

Liz Trippett with Jane Bañez-Ockelford, Daniela Mamaliga,
Payal Saksena and Lionel Vigil

Introduction

EveryChild's projects target vulnerable children who are in practice often the most marginalized and least likely to participate in their family, school or wider community structures. EveryChild's ongoing participatory projects with children in Peru and India have an impact largely within local communities (though they reach further): these include a child rights radio programme and children's parliaments which tackle community problems and children's own difficulties. In Moldova, EveryChild's one-off national children's conference produced young people's recommendations for reform of the childcare system. This received significant media and political attention, though impact at community level is hard to gauge and part of broader project outcomes.

Peru: empowering children through radio programme participation

Background

Research by EveryChild in 2004 confirmed the extent of violence towards children in Santa Maria de Chicmo district, Andahuaylas: 83 per cent of surveyed children reported abuse by their parents/family members and 51 per cent had experienced aggression at school from teachers. EveryChild's project challenges the acceptance of violence as a normal part of a child's environment and pilots non-violent methods of discipline. It helps children suffering abuse to change the existing culture of silence and ensures that victims can access appropriate support mechanisms. The children's radio programme was an initiative taken by children and young people following an EveryChild workshop in 2004 on children's rights – the district mayor was so inspired by their work that he offered a programme to children as a space to voice their concerns and use of the municipal radio station.

How the programme operates

The children's radio programme began broadcasting for an hour every Saturday, later increasing to its current timeslot of three hours, two days a week. It is now produced by 20 children aged 9–15 (12 girls, 8 boys) and is aired both on local radio in Chicmo and across Apurímac department. Every Friday, an adult facilitator brings suggested topics, presentation options and background information to a meeting with the children; the children discuss and select content and do role-plays to explore the issues thoroughly, before finalizing a broadcast script. Content has evolved over the years, from advocacy on children's rights and responsibilities to social skills for children's development such as emotional intelligence for negotiation, conflict resolution and personal leadership. The children incorporate events, music and jokes (in both Spanish and their local language, Quechua), as well as topics aimed at adults such as cultural values and community development. In the long term, the children want broadcasts to involve the private and public sector to facilitate institutional changes in child protection policies and practices.

Impact and challenges

Raised in a culture of adult dominance, the radio programme enables children to be heard and speak freely. Through preparing the programme content with a facilitator, the children develop the skills to articulate their concerns with confidence, discussing development from a child rights-based approach and social, economic and political issues with the authorities they interview. The children now have access to local, regional and national leaders (interviewees include the former minister of health and the regional president). They talk easily with such visiting representatives about how to realize children's rights in society, using questions that relate the interviewee to their organization and their responsibility to address these issues. In this way, the children develop key skills for social and emotional empowerment, and this and their confidence mark them out from their peers; they are talkative and express pride in being part of a radio programme which they feel serves their communities.

The children's radio programme has been recognized by teachers, community leaders and local authorities from the Apurímac region and the Ministries of Education and Health. Ministry officials invited the children to produce an advocacy programme in Andahuaylas for six months to encourage communities to treat the elderly well, and community leaders recently lobbied for municipal candidates to be interviewed on the radio by the children. In 2007 the children submitted a proposal for the municipal participatory budget, supported through a series of meetings and discussions with officials by the EveryChild facilitator. This annual Peruvian budget allocates funds for improving the lives of those most in need, though most community proposals are rejected for lacking clarity and measurable indicators. In this instance, the sum of 10,000 nuevos soles (around £1650) was approved for the children's proposal to train caregivers in Cascabamba on preventing violence to children; this will have a significant impact in a community of 500 families.

There are challenges in this kind of participation; children's involvement in the budget was new in 2007 and both adults and children are still learning to communicate and trust each other through the process. There are practical issues to be resolved too, such as heavy rainfall and thunderstorms affecting the radio station – after the Chicmo station burned down twice, the children no longer broadcast from there during bad weather. There are also bureaucratic restrictions around authorization to broadcast locally 24 hours a day, and the programme requires more structured community support. Despite this, the children's radio programme is gaining in sustainability. It has played a key role in the overall project and become a forum for advocating institutional changes in local practices for the protection of children's rights, encouraging children, teachers, parents and community leaders to work together.

India: children's impact through child parliaments

Background

Child parliaments are not new in India. They have been operating at a low, ad hoc level for various development purposes, with varying levels of expertise across the country. EveryChild's partner, NCN, conceived neighbourhood children's parliaments (NCPs) in 2004–5 through their post-tsunami relief experience. Children were not involved in this, though their needs and problems formed the basis of the concept and they now design the formation of new parliaments. Across the project area in Tamil Nadu state, there is little awareness of child rights and a lack of fora for children to express their problems in villages or higher levels. Children of *dalit* (scheduled caste) and other marginalized communities are more likely to drop out of school to work or be trafficked into sex work or domestic labour through well-established routes. NCPs have a dual function: to prevent children becoming separated from their family or community, and to incorporate children's recommendations and protection into local, district and state plans.

How the parliaments operate

NCPs simulate the structure and functions of the state parliament. Children from each family in a neighbourhood form two parliaments of younger children (6–11 years) and adolescents (12–18 years) – increasing the likelihood of each child speaking, participating and receiving adequate attention. Adult facilitators (or 'animators'), usually women, are appointed and trained by partner (non-governmental) organizations (NGOs) to help run the NCPs. They meet the children weekly or monthly (by mutual agreement) to provide orientation on new issues and problems, and help the children build skills in communication, conducting meetings and participatory rural appraisals. Sessions combine discussion of pressing issues and playing games. Each unit has its own chief minister and other cabinet ministers in charge of different areas such as school drop-out, health, child trafficking and the finance of the parliament; the animator trains each child minister on their role when the NCP is formed.

Parliamentary issues are either introduced by the animator or identified by the children as concerns; the children discuss and prioritize these and then develop proposals to take to the *gram sabhas* (village *panchayat*) or the general body of the voters of the *panchayat*.[1] Animators intervene in the parliamentary sessions only to provide new information, new teaching methods or guide the children to arrive at a decision on a sensitive issue or event planning; the adult sits outside the parliament circle rather than in front of the children. Members then make plans and prepare budgets, adapting the government's concept of 'convergent community action', in which children motivate and mobilize adults.

Most volunteer adult facilitators are also members of the village child protection committee (CPC) and NCPs function most effectively within an alliance of adult bodies such as the CPCs, *panchayats* and district child welfare committees (CWCs). CPCs and CWCs are mandated to protect children and can support the NCPs' activities and help meet their demands. Any child rights violation that cannot be addressed by the CPC is referred on to the CWC. EveryChild is working both to strengthen these adult bodies as a protective alliance for children and support the federation of children's parliaments to the levels of *panchayat*, block, district and the state. Being units of a multi-tier parliamentary federation can give children wider impact for their proposals, visibility and a powerful protective network.

Impact and challenges

Many families in the project area were affected by the 2004 tsunami, and child parliaments played a significant role in the relief and rehabilitation work. An apparent consequence of this is how much children welcome the opportunity to act in a practical forum, driven by a heightened sense of responsibility for their families and environment. Children were and are able to contribute to the work required to rebuild the affected communities, whilst simultaneously benefiting in a therapeutic sense from being able to act constructively.

Child rights violations and long-standing community issues have been identified and followed up successfully by the NCPs. In one village children were afraid of returning from tuition classes at night in darkness, so local NCPs demanded that the *panchayat* install street lights. When this was ignored, the children tied hurricane lamps to electricity poles, and though the residents initially laughed and joked about it, the idea proved effective. After seeing the trouble the children had taken and the value of lighting at night, the *panchayat* installed street lights. Another village NCP persistently petitioned and lobbied their local *panchayat* for an accessible route over a nearby river with dangerous currents, until their local government agreed to lay a new road and bridge over it, at a cost of 5,900,000 rupees (£68,700).

There are very real economic reasons why parents need their children to work rather than attend school, and NCPs have sometimes addressed these. In one village, a girl was forced to work as a bonded labourer after her father borrowed 10,000 rupees (£116) from a mason. After the NCP intervened, the girl's parents decided to send her back to school and repay the loan in instalments, to which the mason agreed. In a similar case, the NCP mobilized their own and government resources to pay school fees for seven children, linking parents to a central government scheme supporting universal education. In some cases, NCP members have organized local processions and street plays to promote an anti-child labour message.

Community resistance to children's parliaments has been minimal; most adults are positive about the NCPs and mothers often volunteer to be the local animator. In some villages, parents became concerned their children were missing school work to attend the parliament sessions. However, they stopped objecting when they realized that the activities of the children's parliament made children more confident and likely to persevere with their school work – and sessions became bi-weekly. In one village, all child parliamentarians posted a 'study, work and play' timetable at home. Parents report that their children study *more* rather than less as they use the parliaments to discuss common school problems and try to resolve them. Community members often come to appreciate the child parliamentarians and listen to their suggestions, such as the *panchayat* members who reported to the project team that even when adults do not wish to engage with the children and find their demands irritating, their persistence and demonstrable results overcome inertia and reluctance.

Moldova: a conference for young peoples' recommendations for reform of national childcare policy

Background

EveryChild's programme in Moldova works closely with government to change national policy and practice in institutional care for children, towards favouring fostering alternatives and integrated social services supporting children to stay in families. In 2006, the president launched the reform of national childcare at an EveryChild/UNICEF conference, advocating that residential institutions be used only as the last resort for children. The project team's experience had led them to recognize the importance of children's participation in developing national policy reform. EveryChild's 2006 children's conference was intended to build the capacity of children to contribute to the decision-making process and policy in childcare reform, to keep decision makers accountable for their commitments, and to encourage children to participate. It was for advocacy purposes, but also to really learn what children thought about the residential care system.

The children's conference

The conference included 25 children aged 10–17, from different backgrounds and with varying experiences of care: *internats* (residential schools), foster care, a small group home, a disability day care centre and mainstream schools. Young journalists were present to help children voice their opinions. The children's involvement had two phases – preparatory visits and orientation and a two-day conference with stakeholders. The preparatory visits included five childcare institutions and services, including an *internat* and a centre for street children. Seeing the institutions had a significant impact on these children, all of whom were shocked by the conditions. One reported: 'We saw that many *internats* [were] overcrowded', and few adults 'participate and really want to help these children'. These visits were integral to the children's understanding of the situation in which institutionalized children lived. In contrast to the usual adult reaction to these institutions, the children really felt that this was not the ideal place for any child – like themselves – to grow up.

The conference itself was divided into two days: small groups discussed child rights abuses within the context of the United Nations Convention on the Rights of the Child on the first day and proposed recommendations for improving children's lives on the second day (aimed at three groups: government, civil society and children). The children proposed that the government offer better financial support for families, organize child parliaments and provide alternative childcare services. For civil society, the children thought public awareness and advocacy were the best approach; they focused on the promotion of a child's right to family – perhaps influenced by a 'lack of warmth' they described in the institutions they visited. The children recognized that children were often institutionalized due to reasons outside their parents' control (one said, 'I think adults abandon their children more because of poverty') and they recommended creating better living conditions for *all* of society.

Impact and challenges

After the conference, interest in the children and their views was immense. The event itself was broadcast on television and radio, and reported in newspapers. A television programme included interviews with the children about child welfare and reform, and the children enjoyed having their views heard; one reported it as a 'good experience' during which she gained more confidence in presenting her ideas. The project team felt that the thorough preparation (i.e. visits) of the children contributed significantly to the success of the conference, enabling the children to present their arguments with confidence and conviction. Their frank peer-to-peer discussions with children in the institutions had informed their judgements and they could speak as 'experts' during the conference, using terminology better than some of the politicians.

The children's conference undoubtedly added value to the development of care services in Moldova, although it is difficult to determine its exact impact in the wider context of the project and its contributing activities and actors. The project team believed that arguments provided by children and youth on this issue would be more powerful than those of adults and it was important for the public to recognize that children with a care background oppose residential care as much as NGOs do. EveryChild's 2004–6 research showed a shift in public opinion on this issue and there have been significant achievements (such as a national strategy on the reorganization of residential care and the creation of the Ministry of Social Protection, Family and Child). Some regions started reorganizing residential care, and two institutions have been closed. Lack of government transparency and institutional intransigence continue to be issues, and the Ministry of Education still resists instigating change. However, the presence of high-powered politicians at the final project conference implied changing attitudes towards the importance of children's voices. Throughout Moldova subsequently there have been smaller child participation projects undertaking community lobbying and advocacy. In 2009, 26 children will be selected across the country to monitor implementation of the UN Convention on the Rights of the Child, presenting their reports to government and local authorities, and EveryChild Moldova hopes to include some of these children on an organizational advisory board.

Conclusion

It is worth noting that the projects outlined above are not designed purely to enable participation for its own sake but regard participation as part of broader programme strategies to deliver child rights (which of course includes participation) within the context of the UN Convention on the Rights of the Child. Their full impact therefore contributes to the wider programme outcomes which fall outside the scope of this chapter. None of the participatory cases are entirely child-initiated or child-controlled, though they enable participation which is informed, creates impact and facilitates child decision-making. While they were not conceived by children, the Indian neighbourhood child parliaments can be (and are) set up and maintained by children once they are familiar with how they work, with minimal support from adult facilitators. The children in Peru had the idea for a radio programme themselves, but sought technical support from adults to design and record the broadcasts. In both these cases, the visible impact of the children's work is greater as they become more confident and reach further – interviewing regional leaders, participating in municipal budgets and attending state child parliaments. The less visible – but arguably more powerful – impact is felt in the immediate family and community environment, as relationships with parents, teachers, or other adults shift in response to children's actions and altered behaviour. These two participative projects have developed in contexts with limited or no effective child protection systems – which both creates the space for children to really make a dramatic impact and also exposes them to risks. In both cases the projects' wider aims involve strengthening child protection mechanisms – which complement or include the children's initiatives – and an overarching goal is to make adults more sensitive to children's concerns. The Moldovan children's conference took an alternative approach: young people were fully informed and supported to write and present their recommendations but within an adult-designed and ring-fenced format. In a post-Soviet context of (adult) state decision-making, young people's grasp of childcare reform surprised and impressed politicians and journalists and undoubtedly contributed to changing perceptions of reform issues. The children themselves reported feeling more confident in expressing their opinions, but it is not clear whether this extended to any long-term change in their individual family or community experience after the conference. As the Peruvian and Indian projects scale up their work – such as at the 2008 Tamil Nadu state children's parliament – they reach wider audiences and at these higher levels of advocacy, children must often navigate and engage with existing adult processes (such as budget planning) which they are not able to control. If the process is less child-controlled, it risks becoming tokenistic and could forfeit the value of the community-level initiatives. Only with great care and ongoing reflective practice can this be avoided.

Acknowledgements

Thanks are due to Sriramappa Gonchikara, Stela Grigoras and Guru Prasad.

Notes

[1] The *panchayat* is an Indian administrative body of 7–30 elected adults representing the local community, functioning at village, block and district level; it has powers to implement social justice and economic schemes and to resolve local disputes, and receives state government funding. The members of a village *panchayat* are elected by the *gram sabha*, a body constituted of all adults over 18 in the village.

Chapter 8

Paving the way for pupil voice? School councils campaign for fairtrade in Liverpool

Anne-Marie Smith

Introduction

[I]n establishing credible school councils ... school leaders will need to be clear that they are ready to involve children in decision making, listen to their views and act on those views where appropriate.

(Whitty and Wisby 2007)

As the UN Convention on the Rights of the Child reaches its twentieth birthday, the inclusion of children's voices and views has become an established expectation of any policy agenda or project initiative for young people. Underpinning the programmes of UNICEF and Save the Children, and at the core of UK initiatives such as youth parliaments, school councils, and children's commissioners, is the fundamental belief that children and young people are rights holders who should be involved in decision-making on any matters affecting them and their peers. In practice, however, such a principle is easily influenced by dominant concepts of childhood which regard children as still on their way to 'becoming' something else, rather than as 'beings' in the here and now (see James et al. 1998; Qvortrup 1994; Prout 2005). With many examples from around the world (as this collection demonstrates) of children's participation in real decision-making alongside adults, schools remain the one context to present the most obstacles to this ideal.

The overall aim of the Liverpool Fair Trade Schools Project (LFSP) in the UK was to increase young people's awareness and understanding of our global interdependence, of the roles they can play as local and global citizens, empowering them to lead and implement activities and action around trade justice in their schools. Using the focus of fairtrade[1] as a practical tool to enable this process, the Liverpool World Centre[2] (LWC) worked with young people who were members of school councils and of the Liverpool Schools Parliament (LSP). More than 60 schools from across the city were involved in the project between 2005 and 2008. Whilst aimed at all age groups, the greatest response came from primary schools – only eight secondary schools participated. As one of five Development Education Centres in the North West of England, the LWC works with schools and community groups on a wide range of projects.

Whilst the LFSP provided a lively, engaging and positive experience for all those involved, it also raised difficult questions about the challenges and obstacles that still lie in the way of effective 'pupil voice' and real decision-making by children and young people. With reference to some of the current wider debates around children's status as rights holders and citizens, this chapter offers a retrospective reflection of our experiences as a development education centre with a mission to empower young people in Liverpool schools.

Background and methodology

The LFSP was one of several projects run by the Liverpool World Centre, which led the successful bid to make Liverpool a Fairtrade City in 2004. The idea of working with young people on the issue of fairtrade was recognized by the City Council as a proactive way of making a reality of Liverpool's Fairtrade City status. One third of the project's funding came from the LSP.

A key aim of the project was the creation of non-tokenistic spaces for children's participation, based on LWC's agenda of empowering young people to take action around issues of social justice. Initial contact was therefore aimed at school councillors rather than teachers. This was greatly facilitated by the mechanism of the LSP where all school councils are represented. In the early stages of the project, this approach did not appear so obvious either to pupils or teachers: the automatic response came from teachers who would then 'pass on the message' to pupils. We had assumed that, since this was a school children's parliament, our approach would achieve the immediate desired response. Our goal of making school councillors the driving force of the project had to be made explicit, with several visits, phone calls and flyers before being taken up. Phone calls directly from pupils ensued, inviting our project worker to school council meetings.

Whilst our project coincided with similar initiatives across the North West and elsewhere, we observed that the LFSP took off with more speed and success due primarily to its guiding principle of asking pupils to steer the project in their schools. However, from the outset there was significant tension between our expectations as external facilitators and the constraints within which teachers or learning mentors had to operate, as explored in the next section.

The initial phase of the project within a school consisted of a meeting between the LWC schools worker and members of the school council. During the meeting councillors discussed the ins and outs of fairtrade, the difference it could make to the lives of farmers and their families, and what roles the pupils and their school could play. The 'what's it got to do with me' question was tackled as a way of exploring pupils' understanding of their local role in our global community.

The school council looked at and discussed the criteria we had drawn up for schools wanting to achieve Fairtrade status. These included: campaigning to persuade teachers to switch permanently to fairtrade tea/coffee in the staffroom, agreeing a whole school policy on fairtrade with governors and teachers, raising awareness and educating others about fairtrade in school, at home and in the local community. Members of the school council then decided and planned how they would implement the fairtrade project around school. Strategies included writing to governors, parents and staff; electing a 'governor for fairtrade' to join in school council meetings; organizing 'fairtrade tasting days' for staff and pupils'; going on local radio; writing to city councillors, and much more. On more than one occasion pupils were incredulous at both parents' and teachers' lack of awareness or interest in fairtrade. Pupils reflected that it 'felt really good' to be the ones doing the educating.

Meaningful practice of 'pupil voice': project achievements

We are so bored of talking about litter in the yard or the school uniform.
(Year 6 pupil)

Without exception, all pupils involved in the project were enthused and inspired to initiate activities, events, and campaigns around fairtrade. Many, like the pupil cited above, expressed their disenchantment with the 'same old stuff' that school council work involved – school uniform, school dinners, litter in the yard, school timetable, recycling. This is not to dismiss such issues as unimportant, but it does reflect a tendency for school councils to tackle what might be called 'tame' areas within school – a wider reflection of who the real decision makers are in schools. Indeed, one pupil commented: 'anyway, the head makes the final decision so there's no point, is there?' For most children, school is not a democratic arena (see Chapter 4 of this volume) and the often tokenistic value of school councils has been widely discussed (e.g. Alderson 2000; Davies et al. 2005).

Unlike requests for radical changes to the school uniform, or suggestions for new school-day hours, the fairtrade project presented a safe issue that could not be vetoed by the head-teacher. This undoubtedly contributed to the project's success in so many schools. It allowed pupils to take the initiative in deciding how their school could run activities, and pupils were able to see immediate and tangible results. For example, as a result of their campaigning and awareness raising, teachers switched to fairtrade coffee and tea in the staffroom; as a result of educating their families, pupils saw their parents take the information on board and include fairtrade products in their weekly shopping.

Pupil steering group

A core element of the project was the steering group, made up of pupils from two secondary and three primary schools. Pupils were invited to join from all participating school councils. The transition period between primary and secondary school meant that the group's make-up changed over the course of three years. However, a core group remained active throughout the project, who met three times a term to discuss events and to help the project team with an exit strategy.

Initially meetings were made difficult by teachers sitting in and making all the decisions! We tackled this by subsequently providing 'extra' activities for staff, in workshop format and in a separate room, while the pupils got on with their meeting. This was received with a mixture of horror and amusement by some staff. However, it also took several meetings of the group before the pupils themselves learnt to shake off the ties that bound them to familiar school structures of authority.

These incidents reveal the gap which existed between our relative 'freedom' as project workers and the constraints within which teachers were working. This relates to the notion of risk taking (see Chapter 15 of this volume): entering the institutional context of schools with a mission to empower pupils could be regarded as a considerable risk. Similarly, those teachers who were committed to supporting pupils' participation in 'extracurricular' activities (such as our project) were perhaps taking a risk *vis-à-vis* the overall culture of their school.

The pupils seemed to regard us as 'non-teachers' who operated outside the norms of day-to-day school hierarchical relationships. This set the tone for a very different power dynamic: we were 'non-official adults' who blurred the boundary somewhat, and therefore caused initial trepidation to pupils (and some teachers) who were used to very clear demarcations in terms of day-to-day teacher–pupil interaction, as illustrated in the following example.

In the third year of the project, LWC ran a day of workshops and activities around fairtrade and climate change, with members of the steering group leading activities for pupils and teachers. For many of the teachers attending the event, being part of a pupil-led event was 'a real eye opener', and despite being vocal advocates for active school councils, the concept of 'letting the children lead the way' was either amusing or seen to be 'a brave option' by several of them. One head-teacher was 'amazed' by what he learnt from the pupils, and promised to follow it up in his school. Pupils, on the other hand, were not so receptive to being 'taught' by their peers, and were not too sure how to respond.

Challenges and obstacles

School councillors taking the lead? It's a bit radical isn't it?
(Teacher, secondary school)

Reference to our project as a 'radical' approach reflects many teachers' trepidation at the thought of children initiating and leading projects in school. This of course varies enormously from school to school, and is often dependent on the vision and will of a head-teacher. When a group of Year 5 and Year 6 pupils presented their school's fairtrade work to a large room full of serious-looking adults, they were confident, eloquent and informative. This was received with enthusiasm and applause, but also with a hint of surprise and almost disbelief that 10-year-olds should have the ability to demonstrate such a degree of reflection around the issue of trade justice. This response, together with the idea that the project's work with school councillors is 'radical', reflects a normative, fixed and adultist view of childhood and 'how' children should be (Smith 2007). To some extent it may also point to a lack of conversation between research and academic discourse on these issues and the practitioner context of schools. My role as project worker was undoubtedly influenced by my previous research on children's participation, and I was speaking a very different language in terms of expectations and understandings of pupils' decision-making.

During a planning meeting between the steering group and LWC project staff, one school council coordinator and Year 6 teacher said: 'You can't expect a 10-year-old to make a decision.' This comment was addressed to a member who was in the throws of generating some group decisions about a forthcoming event. Following the meeting, the older members of the group expressed deep anger that we had 'allowed the teacher to come to the meeting!', requesting that this not be repeated in future. In a lengthy debriefing session, they discussed the possibility of adults participating in meetings, but only if they understood 'what the whole point of this group is'. As a development education centre we had our agenda, which was to enable pupils to take ownership of the project in their schools. Our vision of empowerment of pupils inevitably came up against the machinery of schools, and also the prevalent authoritative attitude of many staff. However, the freedom with which we as LWC project workers were able to pursue our vision was reflected in the way the pupils felt they could 'complain' to us about the above situation. In contrast, teachers or learning mentors who accompanied the pupils to meetings were having to reconcile the tension of supporting our vision with remaining 'in role' as teachers.

Within most schools children have to listen to and obey teachers, take the lead from teachers, and be largely dependent on teachers' 'spoon-feeding' of information, questions, data, etc. The space we provided for the school councillors, and our invitation that they lead with their ideas and initiative, were often contrary to attitudes that they would experience in an average school day. Shier's (2001) idea of 'openings, opportunities and obligations' in enabling children's participation provides a useful framework for interpreting such divergent situations. In many schools the only 'opening' – i.e. commitment to work in a certain way with the school councillors – was the result of a single teacher's dedication, which was not reflected in wider school policy or shared by other members of staff. 'An uphill battle' was how one such committed staff member described her daily endeavours to promote a culture of listening to school councillors, to include them in decisions across the school, and to take their role beyond the context of an 'add-on' to school life.

One teacher commented that, should she 'retire tomorrow', the fairtrade project in her school would disappear as she was the only member of staff committed to supporting the children's endeavours. This relative isolation of such individual members of staff meant that the project's sustainability was often in question. This issue was largely resolved by the fact that, towards the end of the project, 'fairtrade schools' had grown into a national initiative steered by the Fairtrade Foundation in London – providing ongoing support to active schools in Liverpool beyond the lifetime of our project.

In June 2006, steering group members travelled to Whitehall to present a 'young people's manifesto for a fairer world' to Hilary Benn (the then Minister for International Development) (Figure 8.1). For the pupils this was a tremendously proud moment, marking the culmination of their enthusiastic efforts and hard work of steering fairtrade projects in their schools. For one of the pupils, however, the event went unnoticed by the head-teacher and staff of his school, reaffirming his already cynical view on 'the point' of his school council. The learning mentor who tirelessly drove the pupils to and from meetings – the lone advocate for the recognition of pupils voices in her school – lamented that staff 'are just not interested, it is seen as "one more thing to get involved in" '.

Whether the children need a teacher for the project to work in school is a crucial question. There are many examples of child-led community

Figure 8.1 David and Raphael presenting the Young People's Manifesto to Hilary Benn, June 2006. Photo: Liverpool World Centre.

campaigns, but within a school context there are always going to be limits to how 'empowered' children can be.

Concluding remarks

I didn't think of myself as a campaigner before.

(Year 6 pupil)

This young and vocal ambassador for fairtrade made this comment after two years of organizing events with her school council around fairtrade, raising her family members' awareness of trade justice, and speaking at City Council committee meetings about her work. I would argue that this reflects the general avoidance of terms such as 'empowerment' or 'active campaigner' within school corridors; such terms were akin to anarchy in the eyes of many teachers we spoke to. It is also a sign of a broader and more worrying issue: that after nearly 20 years of global advocacy for children's participation rights, it is still not something that many educators feel comfortable with.

As pointed out by David, one of our steering group members: 'It's all very well getting us to participate and lead stuff, but have you thought about talking to the adults about it?' The participation agenda for children has perhaps lent too little attention to working with teachers, head-teachers and other educators around the concept and recognition of pupils' voices and empowerment.

As far as participating schools were concerned, the project highlighted the important links between an active school council and policy requirements such as the Every Child Matters agenda and the citizenship curriculum. Indeed, several teachers who attended workshops run by LWC said that links to policy would be 'the hook' to bring sceptical head-teachers on board. In the context of school curricula in England, LWC's project was highly topical in its relevance to the objectives of citizenship education, the global dimension in school curricula (Department for Education and Skills 2005), and efforts to embed pupil voice in school practice.

The project provided clear evidence that, given the space, children and young people can begin campaigning about social justice issues at any age. Children of a very young age have a clear understanding and perception of what is 'right' or 'fair' and what is 'wrong' or 'unfair'. One 7-year-old pupil knocked on every door in his street, asking for wrappers and containers from fairtrade products for his class project. One door happened to be that of one of the city's prominent radio DJs; he was so impressed with the boy's campaigning that he took his recording team to the school to interview the rest of the class. In terms of children as campaigners, fairtrade is a 'safe' subject that schools were keen to be supporting. In this sense the project, as adopted by schools, represented what could be called 'protected participation'. But it is the beginning, hopefully, of a process whereby teachers and other adults in their lives will take pupils voices seriously and perceive children not as 'future citizens' but as young political and social campaigners in their own right, here and now, at the ages of 13, 11, or 7.

Notes

[1] According the Fairtrade Foundation (www.fairtrade.org.uk), 'Fairtrade is about better prices, decent working conditions, local sustainability, and fair terms of trade for farmers and workers in the developing world'. Or, in the words of one primary school pupil, 'it is all about not ripping off the farmers'.

[2] The author was lead project worker on the LFSP (2005–8), and developed LWC's strategy for participatory work with school councils; see *www.liverpoolworldcentre.org* for further information. The LFSP was supported by funding from the Department for International Development, Christian Aid, and the Liverpool Schools Parliament.

References

Alderson, P. (2000) 'School students' views on school councils and daily life at school', *Children and Society*, 14(2), 121–34

Davies, L., Williams, C., and Yamshita, H. with Ko Man-Hing, A. (2005) *Inspiring Schools. A Literature Review. Taking up the Challenge of Pupil Participation*. London: Carnegie Young People Initiative and the Esmée Fairbairn Foundation.

Department for Education and Skills (2005) *Developing the Global Dimension in the School Curriculum.* Glasgow: Department for International Development.

James, A., Jenks, C. and Prout, A. (1998) *Theorizing Childhood.* Cambridge: Polity Press.

Prout, A. (2005) *The Future of Childhood.* London: RoutledgeFalmer.

Qvortrup, J. (1994) Childhood matters: an introduction', in J. Qvortrup, M. Bardy, G. Sgritta and H. Wintersberger (eds), *Childhood Matters: Social Theory, Practice and Politics.* Aldershot: Avebury, pp. 1–23.

Shier, H. (2001) 'Pathways to participation: openings, opportunities and obligations. A new model for enhancing children's participation in decision-making, in line with Article 12.1 of the United Nations Convention on the Rights of the Child', *Children & Society,* 15, 107–17.

Smith, A.-M. (2007) 'The children of Loxicha: Exploring ideas of childhood and the rules of participation', *Children, Youth and Environments,* 17(3).

Whitty, G. and Wisby, E. (2007) 'Real decision making? School councils in action'. London: Institute of Education, Research Report DCSF-RR001.

Chapter 9

Student voice in Portsmouth: a city-wide approach

Fiona Carnie

Background

Putting students at the heart of decisions which affect their lives was at the core of a five-year collaboration between the University of Sussex and Portsmouth Local Authority which took place from 2002 until 2007 in the UK. Senior leaders within the Authority had recognized the importance of listening to young people in their efforts to improve social cohesion, as well as to raise aspirations and achievement across the city.

The project was an Authority-wide collaboration that included all maintained schools in the city. There were three key areas of focus – student voice, assessment for learning and school-to-school learning. Whilst this chapter is concerned with the student voice element of the project and the ways in which student involvement in decision-making impacted on the life of schools, it is important to point out that the three areas of the project were closely interlinked.

The beginnings of the student voice work

The work on student voice began with a series of visits by the University of Sussex team to secondary schools to explore the level and understanding of student participation across the city. Cross-city engagement with young people came at a Student Voice Day involving students and staff from all the secondary schools and centres across Portsmouth. Inclusion was a key focus so it was important that, at this initial stage, young people from special schools and units were involved. Following this event, the strategy for student voice was drawn up. This involved running a number of events with primary school staff and students to explore *What is a Listening School?* and a series of seminars on student voice for primary head-teachers.

All schools and Local Authority staff had the opportunity to comment on the student voice strategy before it was agreed. In order to implement the strategy, the University Student Voice team expanded to include the Local Authority adviser with responsibility for student voice, a newly appointed student voice advanced skills teacher – one of the first to be appointed in England – and four other teachers representing secondary, special and primary schools. This group met regularly throughout the duration of the project to reflect on progress and plan future work. Student voice link teachers in secondary schools and, later, primary colleagues who were involved in the Primary Student Voice Network were key in sharing good practice across schools.

From the outset the University team agreed a set of values to underpin its work within and across schools. These values, based on an inclusive vision of community and human well-being, held that education is about the development of people and that positive relationships are key. People develop through being part of a community or communities and that working together is central to the process of learning.

The student voice strategy

The student voice strategy had five main strands, all of which developed directly from initial proposals made by students at the first Student Voice Day. These were:

1. Student involvement in governance, management and school improvement
2. Peer support
3. Developing a listening culture
4. Students having a say in their learning
5. Student involvement in the community.

The first strand centred around the development of effective school councils, the involvement of students on school governing bodies and the creation of a cross-city student council. At the beginning of the project only 40 per cent of Portsmouth schools had school councils, whereas by the end this figure had risen to well over 90 per cent. Furthermore, in the early stages many students felt that their school councils did not have much influence. A number of School Council Development Days were held and involved students from different schools coming together to explore how to make their councils more effective and to develop the skills that were needed to achieve this. An important outcome of these cross-city events was the learning that took place between schools. Some schools that had hitherto felt that their councils were strong found out about different ways of working at neighbouring schools and such inter-school dialogue served to strengthen practice in a number of cases. This work enabled young people to forge friendships with students in other schools and it gave rise to a number of collaborative projects. For instance, two secondary schools worked together to set up a student radio programme in their schools, and students from two primary schools produced materials together to support schools in their attempts to combat bullying. These materials, which focused on the process of students working together on a specific issue, were disseminated to all schools across the city.

This first strand of work was also concerned with the issue of student engagement with governing bodies. Such engagement can take many different forms – for example, students can attend governing body meetings; governors can attend school council meetings; school councils can send written reports to governing body meetings; and governors can carry out a survey of student views on particular issues. At the beginning of the project there were only two schools in the city where there was any student involvement on their school's governing body in spite of new legislation which made possible the appointment of students as associate members. The picture altered significantly throughout the course of the project and, by May 2007, 32 per cent of schools and centres that responded to a survey, including 8 out of 10 secondary schools, reported that they had student involvement on their governing bodies. One secondary school reported that the involvement of students as associate members had helped their governing body to function more effectively, primarily because of the need for greater clarity in discussions, particularly concerning terminology. This work was well supported by the Local Authority Governor Services team, which worked closely with the University of Sussex to provide materials, information, events and training to schools and governors.

The second strand of work on peer support aimed to raise awareness of the different ways in which students can support each other through peer mentoring, peer tutoring, counselling, buddying and mediation and to support schools in developing these approaches. The University team produced a booklet on peer support[1] which brought together different examples and drew attention to the research which suggests that all students can benefit from providing and receiving support from their peers – both in personal and social aspects of education, as well as in lessons. The booklet was distributed to all schools and a range of events were organized to promote peer support.

Developing a listening culture was the focus of the third strand – in response to a complaint expressed repeatedly by students that they did not feel listened to by school staff. Based on the events on *What is a Listening School?* (referred to above) which were run for primary students and staff, a colourful leaflet was produced which drew together drawings and quotes from young people to show what a listening school is like, why children should be listened to and what makes it both easier and harder for children to get their ideas across. This leaflet was distributed to every teacher and governor in Portsmouth.

The idea of creating a listening culture within schools was visited repeatedly over the course of the project, and whilst the work of students certainly helped to raise awareness of this concept, it was recognized widely that, for schools to truly listen to young people, a cultural shift was required which would take time and much effort.

Over the course of the project, a lot of work was done to involve students in decisions about their learning. The work on assessment for learning which formed a separate but related area of the University's engagement with Portsmouth linked closely with the fourth strand on students having a say in their learning. This work centred around encouraging teaching staff to create learning environments that were interactive, thereby enabling learners to play a part in deciding such things as purpose, method and criteria. In interactive settings, learners contribute to planning and to feeding back to staff about their learning. Where schools embraced assessment for learning approaches, they saw improved student outcomes particularly in terms of increased confidence and an improvement in the ability of young people to assess their own work and give feedback to others.

Alongside this work, a project on personalizing learning through student voice was carried out. A member of the University team worked with a small number of teachers to explore how they could, through listening more closely, tailor the learning process to meet their students' needs. This work took different forms in different schools and involved students in one school, for example, in designing the curriculum and in another school in dialogue about how homework should be organized. In a third school students took responsibility for deciding what level they should be working at and were thus able to choose what work to do. In spite of teacher concerns that students might tend to go for the easier options, the evidence pointed to students being more likely to choose work that would be challenging for them.

Other work on this strand involved making links with schools beyond Portsmouth that were developing their curricula in innovative ways based on listening to students. Two examples of this were Wroxham School in Potters Bar,[2] a primary school which has student voice at the centre of its policies and practices, and Eltham Green School[3] in south London, which has adopted the Royal Society of Arts Opening Minds curriculum.[4]

Students often voiced their desire for learning to be more fun. Initially some staff saw this as a frivolous request, but with the passage of time and the persistence of the students, some teachers appeared to understand increasingly that if students enjoyed their lessons they would learn more effectively. One primary school carried out a whole-school project on *What Makes*

Learning Fun? and this impacted on teaching practice across the school. A DVD documenting this work was produced and disseminated to schools across the city.[5]

The fifth strand on student involvement in the community focused on how students could become more engaged in community life and decision-making and how local community organizations could be drawn into the life of the school. The University Student Voice team produced and disseminated a case study report based on work at one Portsmouth school and also identified opportunities for schools to engage with national projects supporting such activity.[6]

Over the course of the project the strategy for the Portsmouth Learning Community was refined in response to the interests and demands of staff and students and was eventually reduced to two key elements: student involvement in decisions about their learning; and student involvement in decision-making about school life.

The Council of Portsmouth Students

At the first Student Voice Day in 2003 the idea of developing a city-wide student council was raised and embraced enthusiastically by the students. A speaker from such a council in Norway was able to explain the benefits. A direct outcome of the day was the establishment of the Council of Portsmouth Students (COPS) which was set up as a representative body with students from all the secondary schools and centres across the city. COPS met – and continues to meet – on a half-termly basis with two or three representatives from each school. An executive group is elected on an annual basis and is responsible, with the support of Local Authority staff, for running COPS. Not all schools attend on a regular basis – there are many logistical issues which present a constant challenge – but on the whole, turnout is good. Representatives canvass the views of students in their own schools and then use COPS meetings to take these issues forward. How well this works depends to a large extent on the level of support representatives receive from staff in their own schools, and this varies across the city.

Since 2003, Student Voice Days have been held on an annual basis, the last three taking place at Portsmouth City Football Club's ground. These events bring together students from infant, primary, junior and secondary schools and units from across the city to explore issues together. Students report on developments that have taken place at their schools as a result of student voice work, and this serves to inspire other schools as to what is possible. Not all schools attend, but participation has increased from year to year. Initially, these events were planned and run by staff and students together whereas more recently, as student confidence and level of skills have increased, COPS students have played a much more prominent role in arranging and leading the day.

Efforts are now under way to set up a Junior COPS, though this is more complicated given the much larger number of infant, primary and junior schools than secondary schools. Future plans include organizing a joint Primary and Secondary COPS to bring the agendas together.

The Local Authority makes good use of the existence of COPS as a means of consulting young people. It has been valuable that the Director of Children's Services is supportive of COPS and has been prepared to attend meetings when invited to answer young people's questions and discuss issues of concern.

The aim to be as inclusive as possible has underpinned the student voice work in Portsmouth and this can be seen clearly in the way that COPS works. Students from special schools and units are some of the most regular and active participants. Recent developments have led to the involvement of representatives from the Refugees and Proud (RAP) group and from the C3 group of looked-after children. Both groups have had a strong influence on COPS' work. Furthermore an innovative approach to recording and feeding back about COPS meetings and Student Voice Days has been developed which makes the minutes accessible to a much wider range of students than if the reports were produced only in the form of written notes. With assistance from a multimedia worker at the University of Sussex, COPS used video and audio recordings and presentation software to produce multimedia reports which were sent to all schools on a CD-ROM. These were generally shown at school assemblies or in school council meetings. Latterly minutes have been posted on YouTube, accessible through www.pompeystudentvoice.com. Much more work needs to be done to make COPS – and indeed all student voice work – as inclusive as possible, but having this commitment has been an important starting point.

Issues arising

A variety of issues have been addressed over the course of the project, many of which arise commonly in student voice work across the UK. Food, toilets, bullying, rewards, sports facilities, homework and respect are some of the most common to appear. What is unusual in Portsmouth is the way that some of these issues have been taken up across the city, leading to tangible outcomes.

The issue of respect, for example, is one that has been raised consistently by young people who often feel that they are not listened to. As a consequence, a training DVD has been produced for staff to explain young people's views on this issue and to give schools a resource to help staff work in ways that are respectful of student voice.[7]

Bullying is an ongoing cause for concern and has been the focus of a cross-city schools event to discuss the different ways in which they were addressing the problem, to share good practice and learn from each other. A pamphlet was produced by the multimedia worker mentioned above, working in collaboration with students, and was circulated across the city and further afield.

Discussions at COPS meetings and Student Voice Days on the theme of food have led many schools to involve young people in meetings with caterers, resulting in improved and healthier food being offered in school cafeterias. Constant discussions about the unfairness of rewards systems led one school to carry out a student research project on rewards to gather staff and student views, leading to an improved school policy. The results of the project have been disseminated not only locally but also at a national student voice conference in London.

There are many more examples of issues that have been addressed on a city-wide basis. What is important is that there is a mechanism through COPS and the annual Student Voice Days for young people to discuss these issues, explore solutions together and take their ideas forward.

Successes and challenges

Portsmouth's commitment to putting students at the heart of decisions which affect their lives has had a major impact across the city. Over the course of this five-year initiative, there have been many successes in terms of improved school councils, student involvement on governing bodies, the establishment of COPS, the increasing level of consultation with young people and, most importantly, the involvement of young people in decisions about their learning. Inevitably the rate of progress has varied across the city, with some schools embracing this work enthusiastically and seeing significant results, and others lagging behind. In a number of schools students have been able to have greater input into the curriculum and have been allowed to choose to do extended projects for homework rather than shorter, one-off pieces of work. Furthermore, many schools have drawn students into greater involvement in self-assessment.

Inevitably many challenges remain. A number of people still think that student voice work is just about having a school council, whereas the reality is that it concerns every lesson, every relationship and every interaction. It is about creating a culture in which everyone feels listened to and valued (see Smith's similar analysis of the fairtrade campaign in Liverpool, UK, in Chapter 8). There is still a need to get more head-teachers and senior staff behind this work because the extent to which a school can truly listen and respond to its students depends heavily on the level of support given by school leaders. The logistical problems in getting young people and teachers out of school to work with others from different schools continues to inhibit progress. A crowded timetable, transport issues and the lack of available staff all contribute to the difficulty of enabling students to meet up and work together. And in many schools, whilst there is support for student voice work amongst a small number of staff, the challenge is to scale up and get all teachers on board.

Concluding comments

The importance of dialogue was identified in the Project Final Report (Fielding et al. 2008):

> Over and over again, colleagues who drew benefit from Portsmouth Learning Community emphasised the essential contribution made by talking and listening to one another; talk between adults and children and young people; talk between young learners and talk between adults.

The report highlights the value of having schools in one geographical area work together on the student voice agenda and demonstrates the considerable achievements in Portsmouth. Student involvement in decision-making has led to many changes in schools across the city. Students and staff from different schools have been able to meet, explore issues and collaborate in new ways of working. A momentum has been generated and there is a real sense that this work will continue.

Notes

[1] A list of resources produced by the University of Sussex based on its collaboration with Portsmouth Local Authority and Portsmouth schools is available from e.dennison@sussex.ac.uk.

[2] See http://www.wroxham.herts.sch.uk/

[3] See www.elthamgreen.co.uk

[4] See www.thersa.org/projects/education/opening-minds

[5] *What Makes Learning Fun* DVD produced by Cath Burton for the University of Sussex (further details available from e.dennison@sussex.ac.uk).

[6] Julie Radice and John Parry, 'Learning with the community: a case study from Springfield School' (further details available from e.dennison@sussex.ac.uk).

[7] 'Skills for fostering a listening culture: a training resource for staff' (further details available from e.dennison@sussex.ac.uk).

References

Fielding, M., Sebba, J. and Carnie, F. (2008) 'Portsmouth Learning Community Final Report'. Brighton: University of Sussex.

Part 3

Children as decision makers: what are we trying to achieve? The ethical and political dimensions

This part of the book explores how educational aims of different kinds, and different political agendas, impact on children becoming powerful actors in a world often characterized by unequal social power relations. What are the real intentions behind supporting children as decision makers, and how far can we go? Three case studies highlight a range of ethical and political dimensions in relation to contemporary debates about the nature and extent of children's decision-making in educational contexts. They raise critical questions about what is meant by participation, about the notion of citizenship, and about the role of adults as balances of power begin to change.

Part 3 begins with a critical review of the current literature on the benefits and impacts of participation, and the methodology of these impact studies, by Hiromi Yamashita, Lynn Davies and Chris Williams. Critical of the 'we're doing them a favour' attitude they identify in many studies, these authors argue that children's participation should be appreciated as a highly valuable, specialist input into education decision-making which has as its primary benefit better decisions, rather than an assumed personal benefit.

The following chapter focuses on socio-cultural diversity, and explores how it affects children's participation in decision-making, and its implications for educational policy and practice. Juan Carlos Barrón-Pastor develops a detailed theoretical analysis of the emotion of fear and how it shapes intercultural relations. He applies this analysis to the question of how education can uproot fear of cultural diversity, become better able to promote participation and ultimately make a more meaningful contribution to defining and achieving multicultural citizenship. In the context of Mexican high schools and equality for indigenous people which stimulated his analysis, it is evident that there is still a long way to go.

Echoes of this theme are found in Rohit Dhankar's reflections on experience in North India of the implications of cultural diversity for classroom pedagogy. Looking back on the work of Digantar, the non-governmental organization he directs, in contexts of extreme social inequalities, he questions why the first Digantar school was able avoid reproducing the social power relations of the large context in which it was situated, and concludes that children's participation in decision-making had a major role to play. By paying careful attention to establishing relations of mutual respect, openness and constructive questioning that build understanding and trust, the school enabled children from all backgrounds to direct their own learning and be equal members of a diverse yet cohesive learning community. Drawing on this experience, he argues that India's vast public education system needs to pay much closer attention to the pedagogical implications of cultural diversity, for example in relation to the curriculum, textbook and classroom. This deeper understanding is a prerequisite to establishing norms of classroom discourse that bring about the engagement and participation of all children. Only then can difference be effectively dealt with, and classrooms move on from being spaces that all too often do little more than reflect and faithfully reproduce social disadvantage.

Chapter 10

Assessing the benefits of students' participation

Hiromi Yamashita, Lynn Davies and Chris Williams

Introduction

In recent years, there have been numerous initiatives to increase participation of children and young people in social and political activities in the UK, for example in the areas of personal choices, consumer rights, local community solidarity, good citizenship, and international levels of adherence to conventions. As with other practice and interventions in education, the trend of assessing the benefits and impacts of pupil participation activities has also increased (e.g. Department for Education and Schools 2004).

This chapter considers existing research on the impact and benefits of student participation, and some of the key methodological issues of evaluation studies in this field. This is based on research for the Carnegie Young People Initiative and Esmée Fairburn Foundation (2006–7). It assessed 75 studies, mainly from the UK but also internationally (Davies et al. 2006a, 2006b, 2006c). The review used a definition of participation as 'involvement in a collective decision-making process with a recognizable social and/or educational outcome', and therefore limited the search to a focus on participation in decision-making (i.e. not just any 'taking part' in school or lessons).

Impact of participation

The research reviewed showed a consensus about positive outcomes from a range of participation activities, such as community involvement, school councils, and committee work. We categorized the outcomes identified below in three 'spaces' – personal, school/classroom, and outside the school – while acknowledging their interaction.

Personal and learning outcomes

The impact of participation on learning, achievement and performance is often a key concern of schools. We found that it is difficult to make direct connections and correlations in this area, but the cumulative 'evidence' seems to be positive (e.g. Hannam 2001; Trafford 2003; Davies 1999). Across the literature, there was clear agreement that:

- students in more democratic schools were happier and felt more in control of their learning (e.g. Beveridge 2004; Wehmeyer 1998);
- if students gave feedback on teaching, this had the twin effect of teachers' practice improving and students gaining in awareness of the learning process (e.g. Flutter and Ruddock 2004; Flemish Ministry of Education 2001; Dobie and Gee 2000);
- participation enhanced skills of communication and competence as a learner (e.g. Mitra 2004; Swain 1993);
- skills in specific curriculum areas such as citizenship improved, as well as in other curriculum areas (e.g. Gibson 2005; Kerr et al. 2002; Niemi et al. 2000).

The evidence of any impact on academic achievement of participation in extracurricular activities was, however, not so clear-cut.

Often in parallel with academic achievement, self-esteem and confidence were mentioned in many studies (e.g. Fielding 2001). Increased confidence was particularly apparent for school councillors and others taking a public role. Children with special needs were also reported to have benefited from an emphasis on being 'active participants in learning' and school council pupils were more likely to ask questions and ask for help if they were having trouble understanding in class. Linked to self-esteem and confidence, participation activities were reported also to help children and young people to develop interpersonal and political skills as well as providing an apprenticeship in democracy (see also Chapter 17, this volume). There is considerable government concern in America and the UK that school participation should increase the likelihood that a young person votes in national elections.

Another aspect of personal impact was that of agency and efficacy. Studies reported that students felt they could influence events and school structures, and had a greater sense of direction of their own lives.

Outcomes for school and classroom

Outcomes for school and classroom related to the broad issues of school ethos, atmosphere, belonging and trust. Classroom relationships are seen to improve as part of this trust, as students felt they were listened to. We are never sure if good teacher–student relationships are an input or outcome of participation, but they clearly interact. 'Voice' appears as a theme throughout many studies, and it appears that it is not just the communicating, but overcoming the 'us' and 'them' alienation between students and teachers. The participation of students in interviews for new staff and/or a principal gave them a feeling of ownership as well as leading to better appointments. School organization was also enhanced:

- School councils were able to influence directly the running of the school, with more informed decisions made.
- Student involvement in planning of curriculum and teaching methods again helped in the development of curriculum, assessment and pedagogy.
- Studies reported a range of governance issues that students were involved in: the school mission statement, school development plan, departmental reviews, school facilities, new buildings and safety.
- Students were involved in programmes of change, engaging with contractors or meal providers.

Together with learning and achievement, a key concern for schools is behaviour and discipline (although this focused mainly on students rather than teachers). Behaviour was reported to have been achieved through participation in behaviour, bullying and peer support policies, setting up a peer support group (e.g. Davies and Yamashita 2007), and generating an ethos of care (e.g. Gold and Gold 1998; Inman and Burke 2002).

Research shows also that participation in peer support activities builds on a child's natural desire to help others, and that schools with peer support programmes have witnessed a significant reduction in bullying. Blake and Frances (2004: 16) quoted a 9-year-old boy who explained the benefits of his peer mediation work very lucidly: 'It's as if you are putting the kindness back in.'

Outcomes outside the school

Outcomes outside the school related firstly to specific inputs into community improvement, either through involvement in local councils or through direct projects to prevent violence or theft, or to enhance the environment. Children and young people who were involved in community projects were reported feeling they were able to 'make a difference' in their communities (Hudson 2005). A Year 11 boy (15 years old) was reported to have said:

A few weeks ago we did make some kind of difference by presenting our research and findings about mobile phone theft to the local MP. The way we made a difference was by bringing up important issues which everyone knew about to present to people in power who can make that change which we desire ... many people agreeing means power and power means making change.

(Hudson 2005: 123)

There were a few mentions of beneficial impacts on families, and on home–school relationships (Beveridge 2004). Evidence of impact at national or international level was understandably rarer, but there were instances of pupils influencing national education policy, although in Europe and Australia rather than the UK (Thomson and Holdsworth 2003; Davies and Kirkpatrick 2000). Those young people taking part in participatory and volunteering activities are reported to be more likely to vote in the future and being an active citizen, and there are a few longitudinal studies to support this (e.g. Verba et al. 1995).

Global outcomes were related to fund-raising and charity work, but also to participation in campaigns and protests. Some activities derive from children and young people's explorations of issues such as the global environment or fairtrade.

Methodological issues

While we were reviewing existing studies, we also found many issues surrounding the suppositions, evidence base and methodology for researching or evaluating the impact of participation. The critiques below provide considerations for future work, research and evaluation.

Most studies, even if they appear quantitative and 'empirical', are based on *perceptions* – often self-perceptions ('I think that...'). Usually these are the perceptions of participants and activity organizers rather than other stakeholders, intended third-party beneficiaries, or communities. They do not assess a wider spectrum of stakeholder views, beyond the direct participants. These 'in-house' self-perception studies are useful, but their strengths are probably more that they identify relevant issues and opportunities for developing the specific activities that were studied, rather than that they provide robust assessments of general impact. However, even if self-perceptions of benefits such as 'greater confidence' and 'ability to speak out' are not unambiguous measures of those particular outcomes, they indicate that participants view the activity positively and do not consider it a waste of time, and that in itself is valuable.

Many studies assume *direct causation* between the participatory activity and the benefit (i.e. correlation is regarded as causation). In the context of a diverse and intense school life, this may sometimes be false. For example, can a distinct impact on school achievement be identified if the participatory activity is less than 1 per cent of the time spent on teaching and learning? Longitudinal studies are particularly problematic because outcomes such as 'increased confidence' may arise more from general personal development over 2 or 3 years than from a specific activity. Participatory activities may often function more as catalysts and agency for outcomes, rather than being the main causal factor. However, although a participatory activity may appear to play a small part, it may provide the crucial ingredient that precipitates a significant tangible outcome.

Leadership, both by teachers and young people, is a vital ingredient. But in style it is likely to reflect the familiar sentiments of Lao Tzu: 'a leader is best when people barely know he exists, not so good when people obey and acclaim him, worse when they despise him ... But of a good leader who talks little when his work is done, his aim fulfilled, they will say, "We did it ourselves"' (Wren 1995: 220). The difficulty is how to identify and understand the contribution that this style of leadership makes to the achievement of benefits from a participatory activity.

Likelihood of voting is still presented as a major goal and outcome of participation, yet throughout the Western world the trend is that young people are finding other more effective ways to achieve direct democratic accountability. Abstention is a rational and significant political act, and history may well judge that abstention was a major precipitant of the positive evolution of arcane Western style democratic systems.

The significance of positive *passive participation* is ignored within the literature, for the obvious reason that it is very hard to assess. Outcomes such as 'speaking skills', 'speaking up', 'assertiveness' are lauded; outcomes such as 'listening skills', keeping quiet if you have nothing useful to say, and facilitating weaker partners to present their views, are forgotten. Students might be taught that when they find themselves in disagreement with the majority, one strategy is to 'speak less and think more'. Then if they have a genuinely innovative idea, it will be well presented and more likely to be taken up. We need to be able to value, develop, and attempt to assess the seemingly passive aspects of participation, and distinguish these from opting out.

In some reports there appears to be a *mismatch between the expected outcome and the nature of the activity*. For example, the first purpose of a 'field trip committee' is to arrange a field trip efficiently, not to improve accounting skills or relations between different race groups. Why should activities set in 'after-school clubs' be expected to increase exam performance? Surely the point is that these clubs are not an extension of schooling, but a place for completely different activities. Similarly, is it surprising that in 'centres that operated on a drop-in basis, attendance was sporadic' (Kane, 2004: 2)? Surely accommodating sporadic attendance is the distinctive function of a drop-in centre! Indirect or unexpected beneficial outcomes are obviously worth noting and nurturing, but they should not become an expected outcome unless there is good reason to support that expectation. Apparent mismatches in activity descriptions and expectations of outcomes give the impression of hidden agendas operating in some settings, that is, whatever the stated purpose of an activity the aim is social control and the improvement of school grades.

In general, studies are *uncritical of participatory activities*, and *hidden costs are ignored*. But there is an interesting area of exception: when there is an economic interest such as the payment of private companies to provide activities, or specific state funding. The approach and tone of these studies is conspicuously more aware and questioning, economically and politically, reflecting the style of a formal audit. In most other studies the direct and indirect economic costs are not considered, yet inputs such as teachers' time and administration clearly have a calculable value. When headteachers complain that participatory activities are 'a waste of time', that may well be a rational view, even if it is not expressed in a rational manner. To challenge these 'common-sense' objections to participatory activities, we need good balanced evidence that clearly takes account of both sides of cost–benefit arguments. Similarly, the time inputs of participants are rarely seen as an 'input' or 'cost'. By comparison, when assessing the value of professional in-service training programmes, the salary cost of participants is considered very seriously. Children and young people have busy and demanding lives too, and not to value their time input as we would that of teachers and other adults is contrary to the central ethos of participatory endeavours.

Conclusion

The more mainstream the student participation agenda becomes, the more demands will be put on teachers, researchers and organizations working with young people to assess the benefits of participation activities.

The underlining assumptions of many existing impact studies reflect a 'we're doing them a favour' attitude. The intellectual and other input of young people is usually only measured as a personal benefit – for example, it improves self-esteem or decision-making skills. As a result, there is little attempt to assess and provide critical accounts of the quality of student inputs, and of the real value of the assumed benefits for others (e.g. better street lighting). Would we assess the value of a local council by claiming that it enhanced the skills of the councillors, and not that they had helped to make good decisions that improved public services?

Giving children and young people a 'voice' should not be presented as doing them a favour. Their contribution should be appreciated as a highly valuable, specialist input into education decision-making. The primary benefit of the participation should be better decisions. Young people should benefit from having their inputs valued properly, but both young people and educationalists should recognize that the cost of that approach will be an honest critical assessment of those inputs.

References

Beveridge, S. (2004) 'Pupil participation and the home-school relationship', *European Journal of Special Needs Education*, 19(1), 3–16.

Blake, S. and Frances, G. (2004) *Promoting Children and Young People's Participation through the National Healthy Schools Standard*. London: National Health School Standard (DfES/DH).

Davies, L. (1999) *School Councils and Pupil Exclusions*. Research Project Report. London: Schools Council UK.

Davies, L. and Kirkpatrick, G. (2000) *The Euridem Project: A review of pupil democracy in Europe*. London: Children's Rights Alliance for England.

Davies, L., Williams, C. and Yamashita, H. with Man-Hing, K. (2006a) *Impact and Outcomes: Taking up the Challenge of Pupil Participation*. London: Carnegie Foundation. Available at:
http://www.participationforschools.org.uk/pdfs/InspiringSchools_P1.pdf

Davies, L., Williams, C. and Yamashita, H. (2006b) *Case Studies for Change: Taking up the Challenge of Pupil Participation*. London: Carnegie Foundation. Available at:
http://www.participationforschools.org.uk/pdfs/InspiringSchools_P3.pdf

Davies, L., Williams, C. and Yamashita, H. (2006c) *Inspiring Schools: A Literature Review – Taking up the Challenge of Pupil Participation*. London: Carnegie Foundation. Available at:
http://www.participationforschools.org.uk/pdfs/InspiringSchools_P2.pdf

Davies, L. and Yamashita, H. (2007) *School Councils – School Improvements: London Secondary School Councils Action Research Project*. London: Schools Council UK. Available at: http://www.schoolcouncils.org/resources/research/LSSCARP/

Department for Education and Science (2004) *Working Together: Giving Children and Young People a Say*. Guidance, DfES/0134/2004. London: DfES.

Dobie, T. and Gee, M. (2000) *Active Citizenship in Stirling Council Schools*. Stirling: Stirling Council Children's Services.

Fielding, M. (2001), Beyond the Rhetoric of Student Voice: New departures or new constraints in the transformation of 21st century schooling. *Forum*, 43(2), 100–9.

Flemish MoE (2001) *Participation, Social Cohesion And Citizenship: Involving Pupils, Parents and Teachers in School Policy*. Post-conference report. Brussels: Flemish Ministry of Education.

Flutter, J. and Ruddock, J. (2004) *Consulting Pupils: What's in it for Schools?* London: Routledge Falmer.

Gibson, C. (2005), *The impact of participation in service-learning on high school students' civic engagement*. Denver: Carnegie corporation, RMC Research Corporation.

Gold, J. and Gold, T. (1998), *Learning by Doing*. London: School Council UK.

Hannam, D. (2001) *A Pilot Study to Evaluate the Impact of the Student Participation: Aspects of the Citizenship Order on Standards of Education in Secondary Schools*, Report to the DfEE. London: DfEE.

Hudson, A. (2005) 'Citizenship education and student identities: a school-based action research project', in A. Osler (ed.), *Teachers, Human Rights and Diversity*. Stoke on Trent: Trentham.

Inman, S. and Burke, H. (2002), *School Councils: An Apprenticeship in Democracy?* London: Centre for Cross Curricular Initiatives, South Bank University.

Kane, T. J. (2004) 'The impact of after-school programs: interpreting the results of four recent evaluations'. Working paper of the William T. Grant Foundation, Los Angeles.

Kerr, D., Lines, A., Blenkinshop, S. and Schagen, I. (2002) *England's Results from the IEA International Citizenship Education Study: What Citizenship and Education Mean to 14-Year-Olds*. Slough: DfES/NFER.

Mitra, D. (2004), 'The significance of students: can increasing 'student voice' in schools lead to gains in youth development?', *Teachers College Record*, 106(4).

Niemi, R. G., Hepburn, M. A. and Chapman, C. (2000) 'Community service by high school students: a cure for civic ills?', *Political Behaviour*, 22(1), 45–69.

Swain, J. (1993) 'A vocational special college: preparing students for a participatory democracy?', *Disability, Handicap and Society*, 8(3).

Thomson, P. and Holdsworth, R. (2003) 'Theorizing change in the educational "field": re-readings of 'student participation' projects', *International Journal of Leadership in Education*, 6(4), 371–91.

Trafford, B. (2003) *School Councils, School Democracy, School Improvement*. Leicester: SAH Publications.

Verba, S., Schlozman, K. L. and Henry E. Brady, H. E. (1995) *Voice and Equality: Civic Voluntarism in American Politics*. Cambridge, MA: Harvard University Press.

Wehmeyer, M. (1998) 'Student involvement in education planning, decision making, and instruction: an idea whose time has arrived', in M. Wehmeyer and D. Sands (eds), *Making it Happen: Student Involvement in Education Planning, Decision Making, and Instruction*. Baltimore, MD: Paul H. Brookes Publishing.

Wren, T. (1995) *The Leader's Companion: Insights on Leadership through the Ages*. Glencoe, IL: Free Press.

Chapter 11

Uprooting fear of cultural diversity: becoming participative together

Juan Carlos Barrón-Pastor

Introduction

It is widely recognized that the reproduction of inequalities is usually linked to cultural identities. The *Human Development Report* (United Nations Development Programme (UNDP) 2004: 10) stated that 'struggles over cultural identity, if left unmanaged or managed poorly, can quickly become one of the greatest sources of instability within states and between them'. Education is considered crucial in orchestrating efforts to improve intercultural relationships, but its spaces are double-edged swords with the potential to influence by restraining or reproducing social dynamics. Can education systems avoid stereotyping without coming closer to students through interaction; or hear students' voices if they do not promote their participation? How can people involved in education develop democracies through educational spaces if students are not recognized as decision makers?

Mannion (2007) found that discussions around children as decision makers are ambiguous in relation to citizenship formation, and argued for a reframing through deeper considerations of spatial and relational dimensions. The present chapter briefly explores one crucial aspect of space (its cultural diversity) and one key facet of human relations (emotional affect). Specifically, it explores an illustrative kind of affect commonly found in culturally diverse spaces: fear. This is done to strengthen the argument in favour of promoting students' participation by recognizing them as decision makers; by considering actors as permanently becoming; and by putting forward the necessity of construing and constructing together, through mutual understanding, certain desirable notions such as multicultural citizenship. I consider children and adults not as specific individuals but as members of social groups interacting in challenging multicultural and unequal spaces; and I explore fear as a kind of affect that can be critical for inhibiting or promoting participation. It is important to underline that listening to children, listening to others, is in essence a learning/practising process; children and adults are always becoming something else – becoming citizens, becoming participative.

Promoting participation was a central recommendation to the Mexican Higher Education Association (ANUIES) of an investigation about the impacts of an Affirmative Action Programme to give Academic Support for Indigenous Peoples (ISP) in Mexican universities (Flores-Crespo and Barrón-Pastor 2005). The ISP has been valuable in increasing quotas, and augmenting the visibility of indigenous peoples within their institutions (Flores Crespo and Barron-Pastor 2005), but it has shown problems in defining 'indigenous students' (Flores-Crespo 2007) and, even with the valuable effort of people involved with it, the dynamics of racism are still reproduced within its institutions (Barrón-Pastor 2008).

Approaching affect

Although emotions are commonly marginalized in social studies, interest in collective emotions has recently increased (Forgas 2006, 2008). Affect is the conscious subjective aspect of emotion that has an effect upon, and is considered as conceptually inseparable from, cognition (the way to know) and conatus (the will to act). Feeling is a two-dimensional concept that refers to universal experiences which can be reflected in general semantic terms (emotion); and to certain constructions, such as affect, that depend on the characteristics of what the emotion releases, of its intensity and duration, and of the kind of reaction it may provoke (Marina and López Peñas 1999). The constructed aspect of affect comes from a negotiation, an effort people make to bring emotions and reasons into a sort of equilibrium based on non-linear processes of evaluating four components: the contextual situation; desires; beliefs and expectations; and identity/stereotyping (Marina 1998). Affect is the encoded aspect of emotional experiences, a transactional phenomenon that unchains new tendencies for behaviour (Marina 2006). It is not disconnected from political issues and forms of domination (Lutz and Abu-Lughod 1990), and can be recognized within historical and dialectical contexts (Marina and de la Válgoma 2000).

If affect is a relational faculty humans use to make sense of reality and construct spaces, what happens when spaces become scary because of how different people coincide? Fear is a universal experience: generations which face intimidation, and which are still facing violence, wars and deprivation, show that fear is an understandable and necessary survival tool. Because of our previous experiences as humankind, we activate cognitive strategies to deal with adaptive problems (Cosmides and Tooby 2008) and we make sense of these problems taking emotions into account (Forgas 2008). Fear is no exception.

Mexican indigenous peoples have faced five hundred years of genocide, plundering, exclusion, and currently find themselves at the bottom of Mexican society. Revolts in 1994 against their relentless exclusion from the 'modernity project' of the Mexican state saw agreements made (the San Andrés Accords, 1996) but those but remain unfulfilled by the Mexican state (López Bárcenas 2002). It is perfectly understandable, paraphrasing Linda Green (1999), that 'fear is a way of life' for them.

The construction of fear

The first component of balancing affects is the contextual situation. It is in the constant evaluation people make using all the mechanisms of the balance in non-linear ways to unleash feelings over fields of contexts, which are always contingent and tentative. Deleuze and Guattari (1988: 21) use the concept of rhizome, 'an a-centered, non-hierarchical, non-signifying system . . . defined solely by the circulation of states', to approach them. This concept was created as an alternative to 'arborescent' ways of explaining 'reality', which are 'linear, hierarchical, sedentary, striated, vertical, stiff, and with deep and permanent roots' (Dimitriadis and Kamberelis 2006: 89). The categories used in the process of identification derive from noticing what is immanently different. These identification processes find ways of creating common spaces to define not who is different but, rather, who belongs. The processes of defining are never static and do not pursue 'arborescent' ways of thinking, acting, and being; and they are co-formed in interactions within complex systems. Spaces permeated by cultural diversity offer the opportunity to avoid 'arborescent' perspectives, which are very convenient for promoting fear in line with the current Orwellian 'war on terror' discourse. Such discourses consider education spaces as 'pervaded' by cultural diversity, children as 'distorted' by cultural factors, and people as actors with 'unstable' identities.

Desire is a decisive component of affect which make us aware of the border between what we are and what we are becoming. It is intrinsically related to the notion of power – but power as fortitude, not domination. Desire is not about something missing: rather, it is a complex machine of production (Deleuze and Guattari 1988) and humans, as desiring machines, can attach multiple explanations to limitations imposed by 'reality'. An extended form of promoting fear is the process of attaching the impossibility of accomplishing desires to external objects, which then become dangerous or potential aggressors. When discourses reproduce the notion of other human groups as the main cause for 'our' afflictions, or the main obstacle for 'our' realization, fear both legitimates further forms and grades of violence, and construes current spaces as violent or uncertain.

Systems of beliefs and their corresponding expectations are closely interwoven with desires and socially constructed contexts. Zimbardo (2007) explains the importance of ideology in the analysis of perpetration of evil, and elucidates how impressively easy it is to incite ordinary people to perform atrocities against others if they are not equipped with the tools to cope with otherness. Human beings not only react to events but also interpret them, by organizing their information about the functioning of things. When education, through its discourses and practices, reinforces beliefs that other cultures are dangerous, it creates a logical expectation of those cultures as representing past, present and future menaces.

It is crucial to underline the importance of identity and stereotyping as relational dynamics in the creation of culturally diverse spaces. These processes are socio-cognitive, go hand in hand with discourse (Van Dijk 1998) and frequently produce social suppositions about a person based on prejudices related to their belonging to a particular social group (Zárate and Smith 1990). Stereotypes are based on a supposed fixity to imply the relation of certain cultural or personal characteristics to some other features such as race, gender, place of birth, or sexual preferences (Pickering 2001).

Following Rawls's exaltations of rationalism, Sen (2006) sees identities as categories separated from the subject, which individuals could rationally choose from. There is a risk that these ideas may be seen as a potential invitation to develop capabilities to choose identities. However, the main reason for denying this assumption is its potential to establish 'sets of characteristics' and link them to certain groups of people. Seeing identities as static categories separated from the subject and available to be picked would entail stereotyping; and even authors who alert us to the harmful 'identity politics that polarize people and groups [that] are creating fault lines between "us" and "them"' (UNDP 2004: 11) could be promoting stereotypes by following linear rational ways to approach mechanisms of this kind. As for identification and stereotyping, fear would be promoted through reinforcing certain ideas about those who belong to a particular group, or deserve to belong to it, and would enforce stereotypes of those who do not deserve to belong there. These discourses would commonly attach to 'us' 'good' and 'flexible' notions and to 'them' 'rigid' and 'evil' ones and are the basis for legitimating 'indirect' violence. Sponsoring ignorance of others and enforcing stereotypes can create contexts that Zimbardo (2007) identified as potential for the perpetration of evil through the alienation of one's own identities (frequently abusers) and/or by depersonalising others' identities (frequently victims).

But what if the danger is not real? Then pathological fear can be triggered. Influential groups in contemporary cultures seem to switch on cognitive strategies about others as dangerous or a threat to a better life, and might set in motion mechanisms for legitimating discredit, exclusion or different degrees of violence against others. Power is intrinsically related to the capacity to invoke fear; thus it is not surprising that there is a political economy of fear behind consumerism (Massumi 1992), and laws that are regressive with regard to human rights and collective warrants for well-being (Klein 2007). Yet, as a counterpart to the desire of the powerful to intimidate, fear can also be a trigger for resistance and social movements (Goodwin and Jasper 2004).

Scattering or uprooting fear?

This construction is useful in analysing the ISP in Mexico, where some students in poverty are considered 'indigenous', while others in similar conditions are not labelled as such, and hence do not have access to the Affirmative Action programme (Flores-Crespo 2007). The ethnic criterion used to give academic support differs from the economic criterion used for delivering scholarships based on academic standards, targeting all poor students. This creates an atmosphere of distrust where indigenous peoples can argue that their social treatment reflects an unfair and complex system of exclusion; but non-indigenous students could also argue that giving academic support to indigenous peoples and denying the service to people with similar academic deficits offers unfair access to scholarships (Barrón-Pastor 2008).

This links to the reproduction of racist discourses which claim that a group positioned symbolically below another is snatching something legitimately owned by the 'higher' social group. But both social groups are right – both in this case want to keep studying, and this has different meanings for each. These different groups make sense of one another through fear, as an emotional affect: one group is afraid of not getting the scholarships, while the other is afraid of not keeping them. Both groups attach their fears to the description of the other, to stereotyping each other, and those more powerful will feed the fear to keep control over those weaker in this situation.

Staff commonly reproduce arborescent forms of authority, interpreting the desires of others in terms of the desires of their own socio-cultural group, hence creating stereotypes, systems of beliefs, and expectations about indigenous persons. Participant observation revealed that non-indigenous persons often posit themselves in positions of authority in the presence of indigenous students: many teachers distrust or minimize student's cultural values and may display a romantic idea of indigenous cultures, or a proclivity to judge and determine what is 'wrong' or underdeveloped' in indigenous cultures.

Promoting participation

How can we avoid the reproduction of these harmful dynamics in education? Of course, fear is not the only way to make sense of others. People seek interconnection, so education can be a space for encounter, communication, comprehension and empathy. Fear as an emotion can release other affects such as interest, liking, attraction, or gratitude, and transform current tendencies into mutual understanding. These positive and thus desirable notions seem easier to reach through practising empathy and participation rather than inhibiting it (Hoffman 2008).

Developing participative competences in promoting citizenship and democratic values is very controversial, however, as key competences are defined by the predominant reproduction of hegemonic discourses (DESECO 2008). Because of historical previous experiences, it is crucial to address the monopoly of rationality. Mannion (2007) distrusts the neutrality of promoting citizenship and questions the claim that 'obligation to society' comes from dichotomous presumptions and efforts of inclusion that necessarily pass from selection and exclusion of 'other values'. It is sensible to be suspicious of the innocence of current 'policy ambiguities'. For example, the Mexican government has recently created unprecedented policies for indigenous peoples, but many of the problems with programmes such as the ISP stem from the fact that they were created *for* indigenous peoples, not *by* or *with* them. Now these spaces need to move into more participative practices if they wish to dismantle more effectively racist dynamics within their institutions, and the first steps need to be taken by those who benefit from the reproduction of fear.

Difference can be seen as a positive attribute, for example by taking advantage of many practical aspects of Dewey's 'learning by doing' education tradition. Schweisfurth et al. (2002) argue that creating spaces for participation is decisive in promoting citizenship. How can these dynamics be avoided if participation is not learned or practised? A path for the expression of cultures is what children and students embodying their cultures can speak about; and creating together interactional spaces involving learning and practising participation (see also Chapter 12, this volume). Fear of strangers can be replaced by trust of those who are close if they can openly talk about identities/stereotypes, about their contextual situations, their desires, their beliefs, and their expectations.

People can come close through interactions that occur in specific non-ethnocentric spaces. Thus, deeper mutual understanding might emerge by improving interconnectivity through participation. This calls for recognition, in spatial terms, that increasing cultural diversity is nothing to be afraid of; and in relational terms that cultures are dynamic and flexible which can neither be attached to biological characteristics nor chosen in an identity market. To avoid this it is imperative to promote interaction, not segregation, and to encourage participation, not silence.

References

Barrón-Pastor, J.C. (2008) '¿Promoviendo relaciones interculturales? Racismo y acción afirmativa en México para indígenas en educación superior', *Travaux et Recherches dans les Amériques du Centre*, 53, 22–35.

Cosmides, L. and Tooby, J. (2008) 'The evolutionary psychology of the emotions and their relationship to internal regulatory variables', in M. Lewis, J. M. Haviland-Jones and L. Feldman Barrett (eds), *Handbook of Emotions* (3rd edn). New York: Guilford, pp. 114–37.

Deleuze, G. and Guattari, F. (1988) *A Thousand Plateaus: Capitalism and Schizophrenia*, Vol. 2, translated by B. Massumi. London: Athlone.

DESECO, (2008) Definition and selection of competencies project, sponsored by the Organisation for Economic Co-operation and Development OECD, available at http://www.deseco.admin.ch/ (accessed 5 August 2008).

Dimitriadis, G. and Kamberelis, G. (2006) *Theory for Education, Theory 4*. London: Routledge.

Flores-Crespo, P. (2007) 'Ethnicity, identity and educational achievement in Mexico', *International Journal of Educational Development*, 27(3).

Flores-Crespo, P., and Barrón-Pastor J.C. (2005) *El programa de apoyo a estudiantes indígenas en instituciones de educación superior. ¿Nivelador académico o promotor de la interculturalidad?* Mexico:ANUIES.

Forgas, J. (ed.) (2006) *Affect in Social Thinking and Behavior*. New York: Taylor & Francis.

Forgas, J. (2008) 'Affect and cognition'. *Perspectives on Psychological Science*, 3(2), 94–101.

Goodwin, J. and Jasper, J. M. (eds) (2004) *Rethinking Social Movements: Structure, Meaning and Emotion*. Lanham, MD: Rowman & Littlefield.

Green, L. (1999) *Fear as a Way of Life: Mayan Widows in Rural Guatemala*. New York: Columbia University Press.

Hoffman, M. (2008) 'Empathy and prosocial behavior', in M. Lewis, J. M. Haviland-Jones and L. Feldman Barrett (eds), *Handbook of Emotions* (3rd edn). New York: Guilford, pp. 440–55.

Klein, N. (2007) *The Shock Doctrine: The Rise of Disaster Capitalism*. London: Picador.

López Bárcenas, F. (2002) *Legislación y derechos indígenas en México*. Mexico: Red-es/Ce-Acatl.

Lutz, C. and Abu-Lughod, L. (eds) (1990) *Language and the Politics of Emotion*. Cambridge: Cambridge University Press.

Mannion, G. (2007) 'Going spatial, going relational: why "listening to children" and children's participation needs reframing'. *Discourse: Studies in the Cultural Politics of Education*, 28(3), 405–520.

Marina, J. A. (1998). *El laberinto sentimental*. Barcelona: Anagrama.

Marina, J. A. (2006) *Anatomía del miedo: un tratado sobre la valentía*. Barcelona: Anagrama.

Marina, J. A. and de la Válgoma, M. (2000) *La lucha por la dignidad: teoría de la felicidad política*. Barcelona: Anagrama.

Marina, J. A. and López Peñas, M. (1999) *Diccionario de los Sentimientos*. Barcelona: Anagrama.

Massumi, B. (1992) *A User's Guide to Capitalism and Schizophrenia: Deviations from Deleuze and Guattari*. London: MIT Press.

Pickering, M. (2001) *Stereotyping: The Politics of Representation*. New York: Palgrave.

Schweisfurth, M., Davies, L. and Harber, C. (eds) (2002) *Learning Democracy and Citizenship: International Experiences*. Oxford: Symposium.

Sen, A. (2006) *Identity and Violence: The Illusion of Destiny*. New York: Norton.

United Nations Development Programme (2004) *Human Development Report 2004*. New York: UNDP. http://hdr.undp.org/en/reports/global/hdr2004/

Van Dijk, T. A. (2005) *Racism and Discourse in Spain and Latin America*. Amsterdam: John Benjamins.

Zárate, M. and Smith, E. (1990) 'Person categorization and stereotyping'. *Social Cognition*, 8, 161–85.

Zimbardo, P. (2007) *The Lucifer Effect: Understanding How Good People Turn Evil*. London: Random House.

Chapter 12

Pedagogy and cultural diversity: children's participation for overcoming differences

Rohit Dhankar

The beginning in a small school

Every sensitive teacher in a class that has children from different backgrounds experiences a tension between the values of students' equality and recognition of cultural differences. Equality demands the same treatment of every child: recognition of differences demands 'appropriate' variation in the treatment, taking into consideration a child's cultural background.

India recognized cultural diversity based on languages and regions right after Independence. However, recognition of one important criterion and the urgency to find 'unity in diversity' made us paper over other significant cultural differences. Caste, for example, is still inadequately recognized as giving rise to differences that may legitimately demand pedagogical attention. Religion as a source of pedagogically significant difference in the classroom was also underplayed due to Partition on the basis of religion at Independence. As a result curricula and pedagogical practices remained dominated by a rarified urban middle-class ethos, largely dominated by the values and social behaviour of upper castes and particularly unsuitable to rural and lower-caste children. In textbooks and materials there is not much recognition of diversity in the classroom.

We at Digantar started our first school in 1978 in this general pedagogical atmosphere. The school consisted of about 25 children and two teachers but had wide variation in children's family backgrounds. Castes represented were Rajput, Brahmins, Yadavas, Malis, Dhobis and scheduled castes; in religious terms there were Hindus, Muslims and Radhaswamis; ethnically children were of mixed parentage (Indian and European), Indian and Nepali. Home languages were English, Hindi, Nepali, and Rajasthani dialects. The school was financially supported by one family and situated in their back garden: most of the children were of poor parents working in this family's business, but as children from the family also studied in it there was a tremendous tendency to map the power relationships of the larger reality into the school as well.

The school was based on a free pace of learning and not organized into grades. There were no examinations, and learning with understanding and self-learning were emphasized. Children were free to make their own decisions about participating in a particular class or reading a library book or playing on the swing or working with clay. The school did have a timetable which teachers followed, but during the time allotted for (say) English, if a child chose to do mathematics it was allowed, though she could not get any help from the teachers as they were busy with other children in teaching English. All this gave children great scope for decision-making. In fact, almost all decisions about timetable, school timings, school outings, what projects to take in carpentry and clay, seating arrangements in the school, classroom furniture, and so on were taken in participation with the children.

The age range was 4–17 and in the rare absence of the teachers, children worked alone with interest and the school functioned normally. There was structured space for children to make curricular decisions: although the curriculum was predefined by the teachers, taking into consideration the state and national curricula, the pace of learning, what lessons from the chosen textbook to work on in what order, and which textbook to choose from a given choice of five or six available textbooks was for the children. Such decisions were connected to their own learning and not that of other children.

Yet for several reasons this experience was one of children's participation in decision-making, rather than of children as independent decision makers. All decisions were taken in consultation with the teachers; dialogue and understanding why one choice was preferable over another were important. This made children very articulate and capable of explaining their reasons for the choices made. Secondly, curricular objectives were guided by the state and national curricula; though the textbooks, learning material, sequencing as far as possible and how much to learn in a given time period provided for flexibility and choice, the idea that children can decide their own curriculum was never accepted, since ways of learning and decisions on what is worth learning require advance knowledge of the domain of learning which children have yet to acquire. Thirdly, teachers could overrule the children's decisions if they found them inappropriate; despite large amounts of freedom, teachers believed that they were responsible for the children's learning and were duty bound to help them make better decisions – not just let them do whatever they wanted. No decision was ever imposed on the children, however: negotiation, gentle persuasion and waiting were the key. So children made decisions in a structured learning space, with 'scaffolding' available.

How did this ethos of openness and freedom help in recognition of and dealing with the school's cultural diversity? The plethora of diversity was implicitly recognized by the teachers; the only explicitly recognized difference was the children's economic background. Teachers ensured that all children got an equally good opportunity for learning, and all should participate equally in the school decisions. Fairness and impartiality were cherished values and an inviolable principle; a very strong democratic ethos was established. In retrospect, I wonder why the substantial differences in children's background, and therefore in their thinking and behaviour, did not become an issue – and how the school succeeded in avoiding the replication of the power relationships that existed between children's parents.

I attribute this modest success to several reasons. All adults involved adhered to the principle of equality of all children – an articulation of belief in the equality of human beings coupled with the idea that all children can learn well. This helped make all children feel equally wanted and cared for, and confident that their interests would not be overlooked.

A second factor was the school ethos of involving children in dialogue about all decisions concerning them and children's openness to interpret the world around them in a very active and creative manner. The only way open to teachers and other children to enlist any child's participation was mutual agreement, which was time-consuming but made everyone feel responsible and a worthy member of a small collective.

Sensitivity to each child's pedagogical needs demanded recognition that learning is about connecting new experiences and information with existing understanding and ways of interpretation. The child's existing understanding had to be understood as the only available starting point and no teaching was planned as general instruction; everything was specific to the children's level, experiences and language.

Freedom was available to the teachers to run the school as they thought fit, in consultation with others – including parents. The only constraint was the accepted policy that children should appear for the class 10 examination after roughly ten years of schooling. Children and teachers could use this flexibility in any manner they thought fit.

The small size of the school and a very high teacher–child ratio also helped in knowing each child intimately and building a relationship of trust. An affectionate relationship with children on an individual basis seems to take care of many differences, even if they are not consciously addressed. The personal relationship of mutual trust has the power to transcend differences.

Recognition of differences in the larger system

The pedagogical significance of diversity became clearer only when the single school expanded into a programme for underprivileged children with three schools and about 500 children. They came from various caste backgrounds such as Raigars (very low in the caste hierarchy), Meena, Gujar, Mali,

Brahmins (highest in the hierarchy), Rajput and Muslims. The numbers were just large enough to see the patterns in language, behaviour and attitudes. We were simultaneously also providing academic support to state-run programmes in the very large public education system. Looking at the Indian scenario from the perspective of a teacher with experience of working at a very small scale (and therefore being sensitive to individual attention to the children) convinces me that we should recognize diversity at various levels.

First, it is important to recognize the differences related to caste, culture and religion. In India caste has not usually been associated with cultural differences, but with an upsurge in caste politics (an unhealthy development) the voices of the lower castes are heard more frequently and forcefully (a healthy development, signifying the maturing of democracy). Thus it has become recognizable that the caste differences have characteristics similar to cultural differences. The common forms in which the diversity of caste, culture and religion manifests itself in the schools are as follows:

- *Language use.* It is usually assumed that all Hindi speakers (or, say, speakers of a particular variety of Hindi) use the language in a similar manner. This common language is defined by the locale of the community and the school. Thus one small village is supposed to have identical language, and therefore all children are equally prepared, pedagogically speaking. Another extreme is that a village has several languages even in a region considered linguistically homogeneous. The truth lies, as usual, somewhere in between. The differences do not merit being called different languages, but do mark patterns of language use that differ according to differential caste patterns of vocabulary, pronunciation and intonation. This is very significant in North India where schools overemphasize the use of 'standard' Hindi, which certainly inhibits the child in articulating her views in the class and asking questions: the 'culture of silence' in Indian schools may have linguistic hegemony at its root.
- *Social behaviour and manners.* Distinguishable social mannerisms mark caste and cultural differences, though they overlap with language use. An example is how children greet adults, especially the teacher. Children from many families may not have any specific greeting protocols that they can use in the schools: usual community greetings may not sound suitable, and the farther removed these are from general middle-class behaviour, the more uncomfortable a child might be in using them in the school – which makes her shy and hesitant in greeting visitors to the school. There are similar differences in how one behaves toward classmates, including biases in relation to touching and sharing food and water. Such small things make a significant difference in forming a learning group.
- *Attitude to work, particularly manual work.* Children's family and caste background shapes views on which tasks are honourable and which should

be done by the lower social strata. Rural schools rarely have cleaners, and since cleaning the school may be an unwelcome task for children from certain castes, schools often remain unkempt or children from certain castes and girls are assigned such duties. There are also differences in work attitudes and habits: working to the clock is alien to agricultural communities, where rush periods are hectic but regularity less important. With this attitude examination times might be very stressful, while rest of the year might be pleasantly spent with a very relaxed attitude to day-to-day work.

- *Self-image and identity.* Identity formation is a very complex socio-psychological process (see Chapter 11, this volume); and what teachers and the classmates expect is often coloured by caste identities. Children themselves often have pride or hesitation related to their caste and relative social positioning which also reflects on their own and teachers' expectations of their academic progress. Teachers have very high academic expectations from certain castes, while considering others either uninterested or incapable of notable academic achievements.

Before we come to the issue of dealing with diversity and what role children can play in that, it is pertinent to discuss three key reasons why it is important to recognize these differences. Schools in a democracy are concerned with providing equal opportunity of learning to all. Reflection of one's lived reality in the curriculum and textbooks makes one feel part of the process of education, while its absence creates alienation. A rural lower-caste child hardly finds anything that provides a point of connection to the curriculum; while an urban upper-caste child feels at home with what is being taught, the language spoken and teachers' social behaviour. These two children in the same class get very different opportunities for learning, although technically they can be said to be receiving the same education. If we wish to help the rural child from lower castes, recognizing diversity in backgrounds is a first step; and this provides a pedagogical basis for recognition of diversity.

Secondly, the principle of equal dignity for all demands that we recognize both individual and group-based differences. An affirmative recognition of a child's identity is important in the classroom: everyone feeling equally secure and free in the school is an important value. The differences mentioned above have to be taken care of if we wish to create such an affirmative environment for all children in the school.

Thirdly, democratic citizenship entails openness to dialogue and respect for others. Therefore in the school a proper understanding of others' cherished values, customs, language used and world-view is important for all children. The absence of recognition hampers the development of citizenship values in children.

Dealing with difference pedagogically

Anyone working with the large government system of schools, in-service teacher training and academic support for teachers often comes across the problems mentioned above. A sensitive and sensible educator can often be found emphasizing the differences and recommending different handling of children from different socio-cultural back grounds. But this extenuates the differences without creating bridges and a shared understanding of society. There is also the politically correct angle of shying away from discussing various socio-cultural practices in the spirit of making sense of and understanding their implications in the name of sensitivity and relativism in cultural values and ethos. The other side of the coin is to take certain practices, language, behaviour and values associated with the dominant cultural/caste groups as standard; those seen as lagging behind in socio-cultural development should helped, patronisingly, to acquire the manner-isms and attitudes of the dominant group. Neither approach is adequate. Pretending to accept everything as it is convinces no one; it reduces the possibility of reflection on social practices in the classroom and thereby shuns the important educational objective of understanding ones society and critiquing it. Unabashed favouritism and unquestioning acceptance of dominant social practices and attitudes obviously marginalizes disempowered groups further, in addition to all the problems mentioned in the first approach.

One way to deal with this could be to proceed from two well-recognized humanitarian principles. One is that equality in the school be treated as genuine equality of opportunity and facilitation rather than equality of treatment. The second is recognition of children as individuals, giving priority to the child as human being who can actively participate in her own education; who can deconstruct her own and others' cultural practices and still learn to respect people in spite of all the differences. Thus the child is an embodiment of her own community's socio-cultural consciousness but also able to look beyond this to recognize the existence – as well as the right to exist – of alternative practices.

How can these principles be operationalized in schools with children's active participation? In India children from the weaker social sections of society have to contend with ill-functioning schools and a lack of infrastructure which really need to be corrected before one can deal with the difference pedagogically. However, I shall set those aside for now and focus on three levels where such differences should be addressed.

The first of these is the curricular level. No democratic country can afford to have different educational standards in terms of abilities, depth of understanding and breadth of knowledge among its children. But the same knowledge and understanding can be contextualized appropriately for children from different social backgrounds and connected to their lived reality differently. If the teacher wishes to relate desired abilities and understanding equally to all children, she has to be imaginative, flexible and given a lot of freedom. Since she can never have all the knowledge of children's background and know what is needed to relate the curriculum to each child's life, the only viable alternative is to allow children to make decisions in the classroom.

Textbooks can be deliberately written to make children think, and can present multiple perspectives to be explored further with active involvement of the teacher, rather than presenting deposits of prefabricated knowledge. Children can certainly participate in discussing, exploring and challenging the textbook in their own cultural milieu, with their own perspective and in their own language. They can also be made party to the choice of textbooks where alternatives are available.

The classroom is the most significant level at which the differences could be turned into a learning opportunity and democratic deliberations. If the ethos of mutual care, respect, freedom, equality and justice is firmly established, children can actively participate in framing rules for the classroom working culture. If all the ways of speaking and behaviour are acceptable and the value of making contributions stressed, all will be comfortable and start participating equally. This will help develop a shared classroom language composed of all social strands and equally understandable to all: everything can be discussed and debated but no one can be ridiculed if everyone is understood as an equally valuable member of the learning collective called the classroom. The other principle is to accept everything only when one understands and agrees with it. That would require that all learning starts from where the child is, and if they are all at different places in something, they can all start from their own comfort zone but be challenged to achieve a wider understanding of the issue.

Our practice suggests that if the teacher is capable of creating such shared norms of classroom discourse and engagement of all children is sought, caste difference can be effectively dealt with. I am not claiming that all cultural differences can be dealt with using this approach, but at the elementary level of education, in the Indian scenario, children's informed participation helps mitigate caste disadvantages. This approach recommends children's participation in decision-making but, importantly, it does not claim that children can make all school-related decisions on their own, unaided by their teachers.

Part 4

Facilitating children's participation in research and decision-making

This final part of the book introduces specific experiences of children as researchers and decision makers, focusing particularly on the roles of both children and adults in developing children's participation. The chapters included here provide a range of examples of practical ways of working with children and a range of issues that arise. For instance, as children adopt more proactive roles in educational decision-making in the UK school context and begin to voice their emerging critical consciousness with a view to making changes, the need to recognize and manage risk becomes pressing. Other issues arise where authors discuss experiences of children's participation in research and decision-making in the wider public domain in Ghana and India. These relate to the meanings given to it and the forms it takes.

The projects discussed in most of the chapters in Part 4 involve children undertaking their own research. Doug Springate and Karen Lindridge believe that the process of enabling children to achieve authentic research can extend children's understanding of learning, improve their achievement and self-esteem, and also provide adults who work with them new insights into their lives inside and outside school. Their chapter contextualizes and describes the experiences of facilitating research carried out by a mixed ability class of primary school children in the UK and considers the lessons learnt.

In contrast, Allan Fowler demonstrates, through his work with 15- and 16-year-olds in a UK secondary school, the potential of young people to act as co-researchers along with their teacher. The aim was to enhance knowledge and understanding about the creation of collegiate teaching and learning classroom environments and, hence, wider school improvement. The author describes the approach taken by the students to gathering data. He discusses the range of key concepts and sub-concepts which, for the student-researchers, identified the important aspects of school and classroom life that had the potential to contribute to a collegiate environment. The chapter conveys how both the author and the student researchers experienced the benefits of student participation and of viewing classroom life with a greater emphasis on the students' perspective.

The chapter written by Sue Cox and Anna Robinson-Pant also focuses on children's research, and similarly, on bringing about positive change. It builds on the authors' experiences of working with children as researchers in UK primary schools; the children involved undertook action research in their classrooms. The focus, in this kind of research, on the children bringing about change in their own classroom lives gave rise to particular kinds of risk, which the authors explore. They discuss how the perceived risks influence the extent to which the children's research can make a difference in practice.

Whereas the work of the authors referred to above is located in the school context, P. J. Lolichen illustrates children's work in the wider community. The work of Springate and Lindridge, of Fowler and of Cox and Robinson-Pant suggests the possible scope of what might be achieved when children are research actors. Lolichen's chapter takes this further, showing children's work as research protagonists and also partners in governance who not only identify research needs, set the research framework, design the methodology, develop and administer the tools, consolidate and analyse the findings, but also use the information to solve their problems in the real world. He presents the rich experience of work conducted by a non-governmental organization, The Concerned for Working Children, in South India. While he provides many useful discussions of the role of adults in this process, Lolichen's conclusion identifies a theme, echoed in other chapters in Part 4, as well as in other parts of this volume: children's specialist input has positive change as its aim and primary benefit.

Esme Manful also reports on an initiative that takes children's interactive participation directly into the wider public domain. She discusses the potential for active involvement in social issues that is offered through children's participation in radio broadcasting, describing a project in Ghana where children took increasing control of their own programme. Like other authors in this part of the book, she sees a strength of the project to be the opportunities it provides for children's different perspectives to be heard and taken seriously.

To some extent, in all the contributions to Part 4, the authors face the problematic issues around the extent to which children can and do initiate, 'own' and direct their research and their participation in decision-making. There are questions that can be asked about whether this is more readily achieved in or beyond the school context. The range of contexts provides differing perspectives on the limiting and facilitative roles and responsibilities of adults and invites reflection on how these might be traced back to the cultural and institutional norms that frame the projects.

Chapter 13

Children as researchers: experiences in a Bexley primary school

Doug Springate and Karen Lindridge

Introduction

The child's voice in primary schooling is restricted, and yet a school is only democratic when all those involved have a voice in decision-making both in principle and practice, and are prepared to listen to each other (Lansdowne 1996; Osler 2000; Springate 2004). Primary schools are therefore inherently undemocratic if seen from the child's perspective. This applies to all three major dimensions of schooling: legal, formal and informal (Springate 2004). The legal consists of the laws governing schools; the formal relates to the aspects of schooling directly to do with the agreed curriculum and teaching; and the informal elements are the aspects outside of this. Children have a voice mainly in the informal dimension, for example in playground matters and clubs (Springate 2004; Foley and Leverett 2008). Yet children should have a voice in the formal and even the legal aspects of schooling, something found in some countries, for example Sweden (Davies and Kirkpatrick 2000).

The nature of the voice children have takes different forms. The weakest form is that of consultation, eliciting the children's views about an issue but not necessarily allowing them to participate in the decision-making process involved. A stronger form, that of participation, is more difficult to find in primary schools, with not all schools having a pupil council and almost none allowing the children to participate in school governance. (Springate 2004; Foley and Leverett 2008). Hart (1992) developed a model of participation for children which started with adult manipulation and after six other steps reached the final rung of self-advocacy where children identify their own issues for consideration. Self-advocacy would be the most democratic position for children and would be most enlightening for those who work with children.

The process of schooling is heavily researched, but almost exclusively by adults and little has been written by children (Cullingford 1991; Hallet and

Prout 2003;). Studies of schools have usually ignored the perspectives of children (Brannen and O'Brien 1996). Children rarely have opportunities to express their views or identify problems in their schools or elsewhere, and very rarely undertake their own research into questions and issues that interest them (Burke and Grosvenor 2003; Lewis and Lindsay 2000). When children do pursue issues in school they are often led by teachers and generally focus on the informal parts of school life, such as lunchtimes. Yet childhood is extremely varied and best understood by those experiencing it, so the absence of the child's voice means that we have a very incomplete picture of childhood. What issues would children choose and what benefits would this have for us as professionals who work with them?

The authors are committed to giving children a stronger voice in their schools and in their learning. We were thus very interested in the Children's Research Centre (CRC), founded by Mary Kellett at the Open University in January 2004.[1] It aims to empower children and young people as active researchers and supports a variety of outreach programmes with links to schools and community organizations. It recognizes that children are experts on their own lives, and, by researching topics that interest them, they can provide different views of familiar issues (Kellett 2005; Springate 2005). The CRC offers children and young people a taught programme on research methods, with one-to-one support to design and carry out a research project, and helps disseminate their research findings, all done in a weekly session over several months

One of the authors, a university lecturer, organized a conference in May 2005 at the University of Greenwich run by the Open University child researchers. The audience contained student primary teachers, and local primary teachers and pupils. One of those attending, the co-author and the deputy head of a local school, was inspired by this. Committed to equal opportunities, she opted to work with a whole class rather than the usual Open University practice of training a group of children, often selected from the brightest. The university lecturer was keen to support her. This was a pioneering and brave choice not only because this had not been tried by the Open University, but because the school was in a deprived part of the borough and the class chosen had over half its pupils achieving below national expectations, including some with serious behavioural issues and special needs.

The school work, 2005–6

The authors used Kellett (2005) as a guide to design a series of lessons for the class. The general plan was to spend the first term training the children in research principles and data collection and analysis, and the second term supporting their individually chosen pieces of research. The summer term would be used for the production of presentations and the dissemination of their work.

Pupils were put into four ability groups led by the class teacher, class assistant, and the co-authors of this chapter. Sessions lasted between 60 and 90 minutes each week. Each child received two supervisions from the university lecturer, who presented himself as a supporter/supervisor, not as a teacher. The deputy head led the exercise; as she was not the class teacher, continuity was difficult and key research skills were not as embedded in the curriculum as they might have been. Interviews and questionnaires were more thoroughly covered than observations and experiments due to lack of time and because such methods were more popular with the children.

The sessions were as interactive and practical as possible. The children would, for example, learn about interviewing by watching some role-play and then designing their own interview which they would try out on each other, but principles were often forgotten by the time the children were working on their own research a term later. We concluded that it would be better to teach the skills at the same time as the children undertook their own research.

In all, 24 of the 26 children completed a research project, 22 of them individually and two as a pair. Most were systematic, sceptical and ethical in their research. Examples are:

- Do boys like cartoons more than girls?
- Why don't girls and boys play football together?
- What is the difference between Year 6 and Reception handling their pets?

Others were simpler, lacking a clear research question and less systematic, yet based on original data. These were more like the traditional 'finding out' about a topic. Examples are:

- Pets
- Research on motor cross.

There is an issue about how much adults influence the child's choice of question and methodology. We felt that we should allow the children to retain ownership of their work as much as possible and did not make any assessment. The emphasis was on supporting, not managing, the children. In fact a major conclusion was that the learning for them all was as much in the process as in the products, which included the production of a booklet of all the research projects achieved and the presentation of their work to another local school, including running workshops on how to do research. It also revealed aspects of their lives and their world-view which were new to the teachers involved.

Evaluation

The university lecturer used questionnaires and interviews with the children and adults involved. A quarter of the children said they would like to do more research and a further half might like to do so. Most children thought it enjoyable, especially in choosing their own question to research and in contacting a range of children from their school and elsewhere. The girls particularly enjoyed undertaking questionnaires and using presentation software, while the boys enjoyed the processes of collecting information and finding out what others thought. The least enjoyable element for all was the writing, particularly drafting and redrafting. The children felt it would have been much better to work straight onto the computers with staff editing their work.

Some children felt it had helped them with their school work. Two children mentioned gaining more self-confidence. Some children felt that their research helped prepare them for transfer to secondary school, giving them new skills and confidence in tackling work and thinking things through. One spoke of getting 'an educational boost'. There was real pride in having achieved something which might 'be of use for other people who could read it'. As one said, 'I felt proud to see my work printed. I'm only 11 and I've made a book.'

The class teacher and the classroom assistant both felt there had been benefits for speaking and listening. Recently, when the teacher asked the children for their opinion one child commented, 'You want our opinion like when we are doing our research'. They felt the whole process took too long and there needed to be more time and thought given to presentations. The writing became an end in itself and too often the children were being told what to write to get the work finished. Improved provision of information and communication technologies (ICT) would have helped this.

The second year, 2006–7

The deputy head was class-based for two days a week and could therefore bring together the skills needed for research and embed the work more in the classroom and the curriculum. This work attracted considerable attention from outside the school. All the topics undertaken were chosen by the children. Examples include:

- Racism at – Primary School
- Why do people steal?
- Why can't we ride horses to school?
- What do children do with their parents?

The children presented to adults three times during the research process and at the end. This helped to maintain their interest and did much to raise their self-esteem and presentation skills.

Evaluation

As for the previous year we used questionnaires and interviews. Three quarters of the pupils enjoyed the work, particularly using the presentation software and going to external venues for presentations, especially to adults. Meeting new people and working together also featured strongly. The least enjoyable elements were the sorting out of data and having to repeat the presentations.

Half of the pupils felt it had helped with their school work, in particular ICT and the use of standard English. Also, half reported that it had helped them personally, mainly in terms of their self-confidence. Almost all stated they would like to do more research in the future. Interestingly, three children had not told their parents about doing research and eight said they would have not chosen their topic if their parents had known about it.

Overall the research papers in this year were more clearly question-led, showing better understanding of research techniques. We emerged convinced that the best way forward would be to do the research training and research exercise in a shorter block of time, for example four weeks. Few children undertook observations or used experiments as their methodology, favouring questionnaires and interviews. This raises the question whether we need to explore more child-friendly research methods, for example visual methods (see, for example, Chapter 15 of the present volume). Are we simply imposing adult forms of research on children? P. J. Lolichen in India (Chapter 17) makes the same observation.

We concluded that it was easier when the teacher involved is working with her own class. Similarly, allowing the children to work in pairs and having discussions with adults increases the amount of critical dialogue. The involvement of parents is more contentious as some of the questions the children researched were sensitive family issues but very therapeutic for the children involved. An implication of working with Year 6 was that their experience was lost to the school at the end of the year.

The children researched issues which sometimes surprised the teachers in the school. For example, research by two black boys into racism illustrated that staff were not as aware of the subtleties of racism in their school as they had thought. Similarly, the research on stealing was revealing in that so many children in the school admitted to having stolen.

Facilitating children as researchers was worthwhile but was organization-ally complicated with the school's heavy curriculum demands. Also the logistics of organizing interviews and questionnaires were quite daunting and at times the children were let down by external adults. There is also the question of how young can this be started and the problem of adaptation of methods of data collection for children who are so young that they are scarcely literate or numerate (O'Kane 2000; Mandell 1991). Ros Frost at Cambridge has, however, worked successfully with 7- and 8-year-olds (Frost 2006). The children were very keen to disseminate their findings using a range of media and felt empowered when others listened, especially adults. However, their research needs to be brought to the attention of the change agents, be they school managers and governors or local councillors and workers, if any real impact is to be realized (Lolichen 2007).

Conclusions

It was clear from the pupil feedback that children enjoyed being researchers. Many of the problems were caused by the inexperience of the adults leading this work, as well as time and organizational factors. The second cohort had some exciting and exceptional experiences caused by the attention the work attracted, highlighting the importance of children being able to discuss their work at different stages with interested adults who can challenge and extend their understanding. This experience has convinced us that teaching children research techniques and allowing them to follow their own research questions not only enhances the children's self-esteem and improves their study skills but also informs their teachers about issues in their lives which are not always clear to the adults involved.

In England there has been a move towards more personalized learning in the continuing drive to raise standards and the general shift towards a revaluing of children and childhood, as seen in the document *Every Child Matters* (Deparment for Education and Skills 2004) which provides the framework for local authorities in their work with children. This has included more involvement of children in decisions that affect them, especially in school settings, thereby recognizing the UN Convention on the Rights of the Child. Children's participation is illustrated by the growth in class and school councils, peer mediation and the consultation of children by government both local and central in all areas of social and educational life (Health Development Agency 2004). The government's Children and Young Person's Unit[2] and the appointment of England's first children's commissioner have helped drive this. Children are for the first time formally engaged in the school inspection process, and inspectors judge how well the children are engaged in school and community life. Children as researchers need to be seen in this changing context.

'Children as researchers' goes beyond an inquiry approach to learning – it enables children to contribute to discussions and understandings of their world in a more equal way as they can back their views with the weight real research offers. In this way they can make a difference in their own lives and in the work practices of adults who work with them (Alderson 1995; Burke and Grovesnor 2003; Hallet and Prout 2003). In our work the school and the local community learnt more about how children see them. Yet they must not only have a voice which is strengthened by 'real' research, but significant others must listen and then act with the children to effect change. In this way the 'children as researchers' approach enables children to become fuller citizens inside and outside school.

Notes

1   See http://childrens-research-centre.open.ac.uk.
2   See http://www.cypu.gov.uk/consultationresults

References

Alderson, P. (1995) *Listening to Children: Children's Ethics and Social Research.* London: Barnardo's.

Brannen, J. and O'Brien, M. (eds) (1996) *Children in Families: Research and Policy.* London: Falmer Press.

Burke, C. and Grovesnor, I. (2003) *The School I'd Like: Children and Young People's Reflections on an Education for the 21st Century.* London: RoutledgeFalmer.

Cullingford, C. (1991) *The Inner World of the School.* London: Cassell.

Davies, L. and Kirkpatrick, G. (2000) *The Euridem Project: A Review of Pupil Democracy in Europe.* London: Children's Rights Alliance for England.

Department for Education and Skills (2004) *Every Child Matters.* London: HMSO

Foley, P. and Leverett, S (eds) (2008) *Connecting with Children: Developing Working Relationships.* Oxford: Policy Press and Open University.

Frost, R. (2006) The picnic: developing seven and eight year olds as researchers. Paper presented at the Collaborative Action Research Network (CARN) Conference (30th Anniversary), University of Nottingham, 10–12th November.

Hallet, C. and Prout, A. (eds) (2003) *Hearing the Voices of Children. Social Policy for a New Century.* London: RoutledgeFalmer.

Hart, R. (1992) *Children's Participation: From Tokenism to Citizenship,* Innocenti Essays No. 4. Florence: UNICEF International Child Development Centre.

Health Development Agency (2004) *Promoting Children and Young People's Participation.* London: Department of Health, Department for Education and Skills and the National Children's Bureau.

Kellett, M. (2005), *How to Develop Children as Researchers.* London: Paul Chapman.

Lansdowne, G. (1996) *Educating Children for the 20th Century.* Children's Consortium in Education

Lewis, A. and Lindsay, G. (eds) (2000) *Researching Children's Perspectives.* Buckingham: Open University Press.

Lolichen, P. J. (2007) 'Children as informed participants in governance'. Paper presented at ESRC Seminar on Children as Decision Makers, UEA, Norwich. March.

Mandell, N. (1991) 'The least-adult role in studying children', in F. C. Walker (ed.), *Studying the Social Worlds of Children*. London: Falmer Press.

O'Kane, C. (2000) 'The development of participatory techniques: facilitating children's views about decisions which affect them', in P. Christensen and A James, *Research with Children: Perspectives and Practices*. London: RoutledgeFalmer.

Osler, A. (ed.) (2000) *Citizenship and Democracy in Schools: Diversity, Identity and Equality*. Stoke on Trent: Trentham Books.

Springate, D. (2004), 'A comparative analysis of democracy in primary schools, in N. Hall and D. Springate (eds) *Occasional Papers 2004*. London: University of Greenwich and European Teacher Education Network.

Springate, D. (2005) 'Empowering children through their own research'. *Journal of the European Teacher Education Network*, 1(1).

Chapter 14

Life in the classroom: a pupil perspective

Allan Fowler

Introduction

This chapter is based on a study conducted by myself, the teacher-researcher, together with six pupil co-researchers aged 15–16 years in a 13–18 English high school, using participatory techniques. It sets out to demonstrate our potential as volunteer, non-stranger co-researchers to create a collegiate teaching and learning classroom environment. It highlights the benefits of viewing things from the pupil perspective and, as such, provides an insight into the ways teachers and pupils are able to engage in learning. As the result of foregrounding pupil voice, the chapter will emphasize pupil co-researchers' emic issues (Stake 1995) – in other words, the topics identified for discussion are those that the pupil co-researchers regarded as important and which were derived from their classroom observations and individual focused discussions.

As a result of the research the young people spoke freely about their concerns and interests, and although such dialogue may not necessarily lead to collegiality, it can provide an opportunity for the development of a collegiate teaching and learning environment.

The context of the participatory approach

The study was conducted over a 12-month period using a participatory paradigm. In essence, there were three major cycles, with the first two consisting of six phases incorporating reflection and reflexivity. The third cycle was essentially a final reflection session for all co-researchers.

Ethical protocols

I considered it important to listen to the pupil co-researchers, and central to this was the recognition of the need to respect them as individuals. In this regard, at the start of the study, I adapted a set of ethical protocols from Roberts (2002) which was agreed with the pupils and their parents/guardians in both verbal and written form. As a preliminary to asking each potential pupil co-researcher to participate, I spent time outlining the nature of the study. Not only did all the pupils agree to participate, but they showed enthusiasm and a resonance with the aims of the study. I was at pains to communicate my desire for a cooperative approach; it was not a case of me studying them – it was to be our study.

Sampling and recruitment protocols regarding co-researchers

As the teacher-researcher, uppermost in my mind was the matter of reciprocity of trust, as well as a perceived need to get along with all the pupil co-researchers (and them with me) for the duration of the study.

In a 'pilot' to the main study I had chosen participants at random from my various teaching groups. The pupil co-researchers could thus be described as 'strangers' inasmuch as, although they were known to me through a degree of classroom interaction, they were not necessarily known well. On reflection, I considered that this mode of selection had not achieved reciprocity of trust and hence understanding about life in the classroom, and so, for the main study, I decided to recruit young people with whom I had previously had a good working relationship, and with whom I considered there to be a mutuality of trust. I attributed this latter aspect, as well as mutuality of respect, to there being in part a continuity to our classroom relationship over an 18-month period. Thus, these pupil co-researchers were considered by myself to be 'non-strangers'. In total, one Year 11 and five Year 10 pupils agreed to be co-researchers in the study – three boys and three girls.

Data-gathering techniques

Methodologically, from the outset, the main concern of the study was to 'capture the moment'. The question was how best to do this. With this in mind, my pupil co-researchers and I opted for classroom observation, event-contingent diaries and individual focused discussions.

Co-researchers' classroom observations

Classroom observation was considered by the pupil co-researchers to be an important prerequisite to the other modes of data gathering. The observations, some 70 in total, formed the basis for pupil co-researchers' diarized accounts, which, in turn, formed the basis for individual focused discussions.

At no point prior to their observations were the pupil co-researchers given any formal observational skills training by myself; it was agreed that they would observe and record as free agents. However, in practice, it was agreed that there should be a balance of observations across their timetable.

Each pupil co-researcher was asked to report what they saw from his or her perspective, and although this perspective is itself a subjective one, people in the same interaction could, nevertheless, legitimately report it in different ways, since in some respects the pupil co-researchers were not only reporting the 'facts' about it, but also their experience of it (Duck 1991).

Event-contingent diary

The event-contingent diary used for this study was adapted from the work of Reis and Wheeler (1991) and Duck (1991). It was very simple in terms of its layout, with separate pages for each day of the teaching week and for each lesson, with pupil co-researchers being free to observe lessons of their choice.

The event-contingent diary was used to record data that described and compared pupil co-researchers' perceptions on teacher–pupil and pupil–pupil interaction within the classroom, which necessarily included the numerous small events that comprise everyday activity and thought within the classroom.

The reporting of the observations in the event-contingent diary was immediate, thus hopefully overcoming any inaccuracy in memory recall. All participants recorded their observations shortly after a lesson with the individual focused discussions following within one week.

Individual focused discussions

Individual focused discussions lasted for about one hour and took place between myself and the pupil co-researchers. They spoke freely, with confidence and sincerity about issues of interest, with follow-up discussions taking place during subsequent phases of the study, along with time for reflection. From a personal viewpoint possibly the most important part of the individual focused discussions was the joint identification of the pupil co-researchers' emic issues, in particular those identified by the key concepts and associated sub-concepts discussed below.

The creation of a collegiate teaching and learning environment

I would like to point out that in the following discussion the precise words used to describe the key concepts and associated sub-concepts, as derived from the identification of the pupil co-researchers' emic issues, were my own and not theirs. However, when discussing these during the individual focused discussions these categories were agreed and validated by them.

Pupil co-researchers identified 'teacher effectiveness', 'mutuality of respect', 'social awareness', 'appropriateness of the curriculum' and 'a sense of belonging' as being significant key concepts in the creation of a collegiate teaching and learning environment, where each was seen to make a positive contribution to collegiality.

However, the pupil co-researchers considered that this was only a partial clarification. As discussed below, they suggested that within each of the key concepts there were a series of associated sub-concepts which were also seen to make a positive contribution to a collegiate teaching and learning environment. It was further noted that the identified sub-concepts were not seen to be key concept specific – in other words, the evidence from pupil co-researchers established a degree of commonality within and across the five key concepts – and as such, the sub-concepts were seen to be 'boundary crossers'. In particular, the pupil co-researchers considered that the terms 'continuity of classroom relationships', 'professional qualities of the teacher', 'teacher–pupil classroom relationships' and 'pupil–pupil classroom relationships' crossed the boundaries between all the key concepts.

This section focuses on the identified key concepts, associated sub-concepts and their potential to create a collegiate classroom environment.

So, what is meant by 'collegiality'? This term was mutually agreed upon by the pupil co-researchers and myself during individual focused discussions and, whilst accepting that other terminology could have been used, it was felt by them that this classification embraced their emic issues.

Collegiality was considered by the pupil co-researchers as group cohesiveness, where common aims and objectives are seen to enhance the teaching and learning environment. One male pupil co-researcher describes collegiality as being when 'The whole atmosphere is really relaxed and there isn't anyone who messes it up for anyone else, everyone puts in loads of effort'. Another male pupil exemplifies for me the idea of a collegiate teaching and learning environment when stating that 'You need to fit in before you can relax and you need to relax before you can learn'.

Teacher effectiveness

As noted in the following series of vignettes, pupil co-researchers established a number of sub-concepts related to the key concept of teacher effectiveness, which were seen as being significant in the creation of a collegiate teaching environment.

For example, the notion of *continuity* to classroom relationships between teachers and pupils was reflected in the following pupil co-researcher comments:

My relationship with MT has probably grown since Year 9 and it's probably got better, I feel that I know him as a teacher, just getting used to one teacher, you get used to their style of teaching, you know where you are. If you keep getting different teachers you have to keep adjusting to how they teach.

Another pupil added:

Knowing the teacher, the teacher is really important, it's probably the most important thing. I had the same teacher last year, so I knew her and she's a nice teacher and we get along and there's a group of us that were in the class last year and they all know her.

. . .

In addition, the sub-concept of teacher professionalism can make an important contribution to collegiality. One female pupil co-researcher considered that this is more likely to happen when:

The teacher includes you in the lesson as well, that helps, you just feel comfortable and you haven't got to worry then.

She added:

The lesson is taken seriously, but in a fun way ... the teacher has a laugh with you as well, while you're getting on with the work, which makes it fun.

In addition, one pupil co-researcher considered that it is important for a teacher to be a subject-specialist:

I always feel good going to English, there's a big feel good factor. Have loads of friends and really like Miss —————'s teaching methods, always know what's going on, never confused.

Another pupil added:

The teacher was interested in the subject, and we were interested in the subject, so instead of having to be kept told off there was an amount of relaxed attitude towards it, the work still got done in that lesson.

Mutuality of respect

Turning now to the second key concept, pupil co-researchers noted that, within a teaching group, collegiality is more likely to occur where there is mutuality of respect between the pupils themselves, as one female pupil co-researcher described:

> Yourself and the other people in the group, you need to respect them and they'll respect you back, which makes it a comfortable situation to be in.

One male pupil co-researcher attributed this latter aspect to continuity in the relationship between the pupils themselves in a teaching group:

> A lot of people knew each other before they went in there, which helps, either from year nine or middle school.

However, it was also noted that an effective teaching and learning environment could be compromised where mutuality of respect between a teacher and pupils was not evident, as one female pupil co-researcher stated:

> I dislike teachers that demand your respect, that don't feel that they have to give any back and I feel that there should be equal amounts of respect.

Pupil co-researchers also considered that mutuality of respect was more likely to make a contribution to collegiality when the key concept of social awareness (discussed next) was also making a contribution. Hence social awareness can be regarded as an important antecedent to that of mutuality of respect and as such highlights the idea of interconnectedness (discussed later).

Social awareness

The study demonstrated a link between high levels of social awareness and collegiality. In the words of one female pupil:

> If everyone [the pupils] gets on with everyone else, then it's going to make for a more comfortable life.

Another pupil supported this, adding:

> Most of them [the pupils] are aware of other people's feelings ... yes we get the education we want and it's mostly in a friendly atmosphere.

This seems to suggest that some young people have, in fact, developed social awareness, or what Sants (1984) refers to as 'social accommodation' and so they are able to understand that people have different personalities and ways of interacting, and that to maximize success in relationships, these differences must be accommodated.

Appropriateness of the curriculum

Another aspect to the story being told by pupil co-researchers about life in a collegiate classroom relates to the key concept of appropriateness of the curriculum. Within this key concept they highlighted the sub-concept of 'pupil interest in a subject', arguing that it has the potential to make an important contribution to the creation of an effective teaching and learning environment. As one male pupil put it:

> The only thing you need in a lesson like drama is for everyone to be interested in the subject you are doing. If you get a subject like French for instance, there are a couple of people that are interested in it, but not everyone is, so the group is split into sub-groups rather than work ethic.

Another added:

> [English] is probably my favourite lesson out of them all really, this is the one that I really, really enjoy going to, I really fit in and can really excel in this lesson. I like it and I'm hoping to go into a career in it.

The above is seen to demonstrate this sub-concept as having the potential to make a positive contribution to collegiality. One pupil co-researcher raised the possibility of the negative impact of lack of interest:

> Some people don't want to do history, but you have to make a choice between history and geography and some don't want to do either.

Another seemed to confirm this:

> I picked history because I didn't like geography, but I didn't want to do either.

Sense of belonging

A sense of belonging, and specifically a need to feel part of a teaching group, is seen to enhance self-esteem and self-confidence, which, as one female co-researcher noted, encouraged her to speak in a debate and take part in role-play:

> I love English, I feel part of the group and have loads of friends. We had speaking and listening, we acted and had a good time.

Another pupil co-researcher wrote:

I really enjoyed this lesson [RE] somehow we ended up debating dictatorships, I love political debates. I really felt good during this, it's the theory of feeding off others' energy.

Another pupil co-researcher found that a sense of belonging, supplemented by a keen interest in a subject and a feel-good factor, provided a stimulus for the continued enhancement of personal self-esteem:

My self-esteem is quite high, ever since I started doing art at school. ... everyone always says that I'm good at it, so that sort of encourages me.

The above draws our attention to the idea of interconnectedness within and among identified key concepts and associated sub-concepts.

The idea of interconnectedness

Like Bany and Johnson (1964), pupil co-researchers highlighted the importance of developing a good feeling about the teaching group as a whole, even though each individual member may not hold strong feelings of friendship for others in the class. But Bany and Johnson consider that although this concept is frequently stressed in education there is very little understanding about the determinants of this condition.

Pertinent to this, the evidence from pupil co-researchers, as discussed above, has highlighted a number of key concepts or determinants as being potentially significant in the creation of a collegiate teaching and learning environment. However, this was once again considered to be only a partial clarification, as it was noted that throughout the above discussions pupil co-researchers found it difficult to talk about an individual key concept and associated sub-concepts without involving to a greater or lesser degree some or all of the others, and in so doing, highlighted the idea of interconnectedness within and among the key concepts.

The pupil co-researchers considered that understanding of the concept of collegiality had been derived not so much from the individual key concepts themselves, but more in the nature of their interconnectedness within and among the others. Thus, in order to understand the whole in the form of collegiality, it is necessary to understand the parts, in the form of the individual key concepts and associated sub-concepts. Geertz (1975: 52–3) illustrates this well when he says:

Hopping back and forth between the whole, conceived through the parts which actualise it and the parts conceived through the whole which motivates them, we seek to turn them, by a sort of intellectual perpetual motion, into explications of one another.

Hence, in relation to collegiality, compartmentalizing teacher effectiveness, mutuality of respect, social awareness, appropriateness of the curriculum and ignoring a need to belong is inappropriate, artificial and misleading. Indeed, like Moss (1998), the findings of this study are seen to support the idea of collegiality being conceptualized as interlocking building blocks forming the foundation for meaningful learning.

Conclusion

This chapter has, I believe, demonstrated the benefit of viewing learning in the classroom from the pupil perspective. In so doing, it has highlighted a series of key concepts and associated sub-concepts which were seen by the pupil co-researchers to have the potential to develop a collegiate teaching and learning environment. In addition, they drew attention to the idea of interconnectedness within and among the key concepts and associated sub-concepts. Our understanding, therefore, of a collegiate teaching and learning environment should go beyond the notion of separate entities, in the form of individual key concepts, to a recognition of this interconnectedness.

The realization of a need to listen to pupil voice has provided me with an insight into the ways teachers and pupils are able to engage in learning and, as such, I would respectfully encourage others to adopt similar participatory approaches as an aid to meaningful reflection on classroom practice.

References

Bany, M. and Johnson, L. (1964) *Classroom Group Behavior: Group Dynamics in Education*. New York: Macmillan.

Duck, S. (1991) 'Diaries and logs', in B. Montgomery and S. Duck (eds), *Studying Social Interaction*. New York: Guilford Press.

Geertz, C. (1975) 'On the nature of anthropological understanding'. *American Scientist*, 63, 47–53.

Moss, G. (1998) 'Coaching pupils to behave', *Managing Schools Today*, 8, 3, 27–28.

Reis, H. and Wheeler, L. (1991) 'Studying social interaction with the Rochester Interaction Record'. *Advances in Experimental Social Psychology*, 24, 269–318.

Roberts, H. (2002) 'Listening to children: and hearing them', in P. Christensen and A. James (eds), *Research with Children: Perspectives and Practices*. London: Routledge.

Sants, H. (1984) 'Conceptions of friendship, social behaviour and school achievement in six-year-old children'. *Journal of Social and Personal Relationships*, 1, 293–309.

Stake, R. (1995) *The Art of Case Study Research*. London: Sage.

Chapter 15

Children as *researchers: a question of risk?*

Sue Cox and Anna Robinson-Pant

Introduction

Building on our experiences of working with children as researchers in English primary schools, in this chapter we discuss the question of risk taking and its wider implications. Our own project has revealed that when children are active researchers, teachers encounter and perceive different kinds of risks which have implications for children's participation in research and decision-making. The chapter explores the constraints and opportunities around risk taking which affected the children's research.

Working with children as action researchers in school: two dimensions of risk

Our interest in discussing the question of risk arises from the work we have been engaged in that involves children as researchers and decision makers. Two dimensions of risk emerged from this work. The first was related to the particular conceptions and assumptions about childhood that were shared by adults in our research team. As we worked on the project, it became clear that we were engaging with ideas about children's needs for adult care and protection from responsibilities (one responsibility being the need to make their own decisions). This may differ from other cultural contexts described in this book, where, for example, children may be expected to contribute to household income through paid labour.

The second dimension of risk arose from working with children and teachers in schools. We found that this institutional context shaped our research activities in ways that might differ from conducting research in other kinds of communities and institutions. (In Chapter 17, Lolichen discusses young people conducting research as part of a project facilitated by an NGO in India, The Concerned for Working Children.) There are particular parameters related to school and educational cultures which have an impact on how teachers and children act. For instance, national and local policy frameworks influence teachers' and students' expectations of both activities and relationships between adults and children within the school environment. One consequence of this is that children would expect teachers to take the lead in decision-making and teachers would see it as their responsibility to determine the direction of children's activities, at least to the extent of meeting their professional obligations as educators. In the current educational climate in England (as in many other countries) there has been a strong emphasis on children's attainment and performance against national benchmarks (see Chapter 1 in this volume). There are signs that this is changing – currently the Primary Review (see Department for Children, Schools and Families 2008) being undertaken in England is considering new models of curriculum, and the increasing emphasis on children's rights and roles as citizens in educational programmes is shifting the balance. However, it is likely that the hierarchical relationships between adults and children associated with schools will be difficult to shift. Certainly, our own work carried out in Norfolk schools in 2004–6 suggested that at that time, these power relations created particular constraints on children acting as action researchers.

The project, 'Children Decide: Power, participation and purpose in the primary classroom', was carried out by children and teachers in nine Norfolk classrooms, in collaboration with ourselves as university-based researchers. The project involved children researching their own decision-making with the aim of bringing about change and finding new opportunities for collaborating with their teachers in making decisions. There was an understanding from the start that there were constraints on fully handing over control of decision-making to children. We had already revealed the effect of implicit power relationships in an earlier project, 'Empowering Children through Visual Communication' (Cox et al. 2003), and the limitations they imposed. We were concerned to encourage children to become more aware of 'the potential for renegotiating the limits to their power with teachers, other children and other parties' whilst acknowledging the 'non-negotiable constraints which limit their power (e.g. statutory curriculum, legal governance of schools) and the potential for questioning these' (Cox et al. 2006: 12).

Like Doug Springate and Karen Lindridge (Chapter 13 of the present volume), we adopted a whole-class approach rather than identifying a small group of students to conduct the research. However, our approach differed in that we had determined that the general research focus would be on decision-making (in contrast to the children at the primary school where Springate and Lindridge worked, who decided their own individual research questions). On the other hand, our research focus in itself was intended to give children greater control over their lives in schools and provide the opportunity to effect change. This was achieved through introducing the model of action research based on cycles of action and reflection. The cycles began with 'reconnaissance' (researching decision-making already going on in their classrooms/ schools) and led into action planning (children and teachers deciding changes that they would like to make to classroom practices) then evaluation of the outcomes. Each class developed their own research design. As well as using methods such as interviews and questionnaires, they drew on visual and practical approaches (introduced by the teachers and university researchers) intended to enhance children's participation in data collection and analysis.

Perceptions of risk: the limitations for action research

As university researchers, we saw action research as a powerful means for children to effect change. Perhaps what we had not fully anticipated was the effect on the project of the existing framework of assumptions within which teachers and children work. This created tacit boundaries beyond which both teachers and children perceived risk related to the two dimensions discussed above. One of the clear examples of this was the difficulty faced by many of the teachers in moving from the reconnaissance stage of the action research into planning and creating change. Teachers appeared to feel safer encouraging children to find out and report on decision-making already going on in their lives and their classrooms. It was perhaps more straightforward to involve the children in collecting this kind of data, as it was consistent with normal classroom activity. The children gathered information and discussed who made decisions and when in a typical school day and at home – for instance, through constructing timelines, children identified the different activities in their day and used counters to indicate the situations when they made decisions for themselves (more counters for more decisions). They also mapped out the extent to which various members of the school community made decisions through 'institutional diagrams'. Paper circles were cut in different sizes ('the bigger the circle, the bigger the say') and placed in relationship to each other to represent the importance of the decision maker and their interaction with others.

Clearly teachers and children were working in familiar ways here. The teachers were keen to adopt the participatory approaches to 'finding out', and to encourage the children to lead in these activities, but the further step of engaging in negotiation with the children on their ideas for action may have been perceived to be more of a risk. As a Year 4 teacher commented: 'To hand over this responsibility was at first a daunting and foreboding experience for both the children and me' (White 2006: 172). From the teacher's perspective – working in a world where curriculum and attainment targets must be met, time is short and colleagues may have differing ideas about 'pupil participation' – there were compelling reasons for staying in charge of decision-making. Teachers were keen to encourage children to learn how to do research, and this would come within the inquiry-based learning that underpins much of the national curriculum in England. However, action research demands more than this, implying an emphasis on change by and for the participants. This tension reflects similar debates in citizenship education – about how far the emphasis should be on learning about citizenship for the future, as compared to being active child citizens (Rudduck 2003).

The teachers' reasoning was not just reactive to the situations they found themselves in but reflected their aims as educators; they were concerned to ensure that children's learning experiences were worthwhile (see Chapter 12 of the present volume for discussion of related issues). They were aware that some of the decisions that children felt were important could be considered 'trivial' from an adult perspective – such as which pen they chose, where they sat on the carpet and who they played with – which at face value, did not seem important in educational terms. There was also the worry about children failing if they set out to do something too ambitious – in our meetings, a teacher observed: 'I'm just anxious what the children are going to think at the end of it [the project] – worried they will feel they haven't achieved a lot considering the amount of work and time and effort they spent on it – just going to think, Miss could have done that' (Cox et al. 2006: 31). This kind of reasoning is framed by the first dimension of risk taking mentioned above – the dominant conceptions of childhood which position teachers as protectors and guides, emphasized by one of the teachers: 'Perhaps this is a valuable part of childhood, that children are free from having to make decisions, something that will present itself all too readily once they become adults' (Millner 2006: 70). Similarly, in relation to the second dimension of risk, the teachers' pedagogical principles would include a commitment to promoting children's self-esteem (through avoiding experiences of failure).

Once the research moved into the action-planning and decision-making phase, the teachers had to engage with these issues more directly. There was the potential here for children to become disappointed and disillusioned when the changes that they proposed were apparently non-negotiable. This caused the teachers to face what was non-negotiable and what was not. For instance, in one school, children wanted to make choices about their writing style but there was a school-wide handwriting policy that prevented this. In another school, children were unhappy with the ability-based maths classes ('setting'). By discovering through interviews with their peers what the children's real feelings were, the child researchers ran the risk of conflict with their teachers who had a different rationale for the decisions.

The fact that we had decided to adopt an action research approach, rather than conventional empirical research or investigation, made the risks of working with children as researchers more visible. This created dilemmas within the research process, especially for teachers, about whether they could actually carry through the changes proposed by the children.

Teachers as experts?

One thing that this kind of research highlighted for the teachers was the way they interpreted children's needs, as compared to the children's actual felt needs. If teachers were to take children's wants and needs seriously, this could create difficulties for them in their role as the 'authority' in the classroom. Several teachers in the project addressed this by encouraging children to reflect on pros and cons when researching possibilities for change. For instance, a Year 1 class wanted to have animals in the classroom because 'people will have fun', 'get to know animals', 'get to stroke animals'. Looking at the disadvantages, the children noted that: 'people would get ill', 'catch diseases', 'not play with toys', 'have to clean up the room', the animals 'might chew on things', and would 'poo on your body'. The teacher in this class felt that children would see from this process which 'changes would be the most workable in the first instance, and which would not be practical' (Jarvis and Frederick 2006: 118). This process of reasoning seemed to help the children recognize an adult point of view on their suggestions. Where the adult is seen as the expert and the arbiter of knowledge – as may be the case in classrooms in the current UK educational climate – this would be seen as good educational practice.

The teachers in the project recognized the changes in their own practice and attitudes that were called for when adults shared their reasoning with children. At the end of the project, they commented:

> we all found we were more willing to explain the reasons for the decisions we routinely made. Children began to ask 'why?' for explanation ... As teachers we found we were involving children more in the decisions we made and talking about things together. As a consequence we found that children were more able to identify, understand, and empathise with the reasoning behind our decisions.
>
> (Cox et al. 2007: 29)

Occasionally, children's reasoning led them to a different conclusion from the teacher. For example, in the situation noted above, when the children expressed their views about 'setting' for maths, this conflicted with the teachers' plans which were influenced by national recommendations and created dilemmas for them as organizers of learning (Taylor 2006). Children felt very strongly about the issue, and had reasons of their own for preferring an alternative arrangement. Similarly, in a Year 6 class, the children decided on the basis of their research that they would like to introduce lessons taught by themselves. Their teacher faced the dilemma of how to reconcile this with his own priorities which included ensuring that they were successful in meeting school targets in standard attainment tests (SATs). His solution was to offer the children the opportunity to run these lessons, but only within a 45-minute time slot each week.

The teachers recognized that to allow the children any more control over the curriculum would entail a different level of risk as it would present a challenge to the current institutional practices. These examples raise the question as to whose reasoning was most valid and how to resolve conflicting interests. It demanded at least that children were taken into teachers' confidence about the reasons for adult decisions. As a Year 1 teacher reported, 'An important aspect of empowerment and participation for me is ... explaining and helping children understand what decisions I make and why I make them' (Lawes 2006: 59). Taken further, it would require that children's arguments should carry equal weight. In reflecting back on the project, the Year 6 teacher above noted a shift in the balance of power in his classroom:

> I began to consider how many decisions I was needlessly making for the children and began looking much more for opportunities for the children to make more meaningful decisions which involved thinking and reasoning. ... The relationship between the children and myself became much more of a partnership with the feeling that education was not done to my students but with them.
>
> (Currie 2006: 195)

This was a move toward sharing control with the children, accepting the risks discussed earlier in relation to the specific institutional context of school. Whilst this teacher has acknowledged the challenges to his power, it would be a further step to accept that children's reasoning counts for as much as that of their teachers. The latter would imply that teachers and children through their research are co-constructors of knowledge rather than the teacher being the ultimate authority or 'expert'. During the project, there were several occasions when teachers reflected on the knowledge they had gained through the children's action research. For instance, a Year 6 teacher discussed children's analysis of 'where, when, what and how we learn', commenting: 'these children produced some thought-provoking work that again made the teacher reflect upon the classroom environment as a centre for learning' (Jarvis and Frederick 2006: 120). Similarly, a Year 4 teacher came to see the possible extent of children's contribution in a different way: 'I very quickly realized that the sheer quantity of everyday decisions and my justifications were largely inaccessible to the children. In opening up this process it became very apparent that the children could easily understand, partake in, succeed in and benefit from making their own effective decisions' (White 2006: 172).

As the project progressed, we became aware how strongly children's assumptions about their roles and relationships with adults were influenced by the institution of the school. In the reconnaissance phase of the project, the teachers promoted opportunities to disrupt these expectations. For instance, a Year 2 teacher set up a scenario where she took complete control (even over decisions the children would normally make for themselves, such as where to sit and choosing their reading books) in order to stimulate discussion about children's expectations of roles within the classroom. In discussion, the children acknowledged that they had conformed to this unusual situation without complaint. The teacher commented 'they explained by saying they thought I would tell them off' (Stubbs 2006: 83). This situation led the children to point out that the teacher's power was not absolute: 'if you make bad decisions like torture us, we'll phone the police' (Cox et al. 2006: 31). Whilst the children could recognize this in a hypothetical situation, in the context of the teacher's 'bossy day' (the children's words), it was clear that they were not prepared to challenge the teacher's authority. In the Year 6 class (see above), the children came up with a list of ways in which they learned (including 'reading, watching television, learning from our mistakes, cooperation with others, learning from experience'). However, their research also revealed that 'many children believed that other people, namely the teacher, headteacher, governors and the government are in charge of how they learn' (Jarvis and Frederick 2006: 121).

At the beginning of the project, we had noted that 'children rarely reported making decisions that directly affected their learning and [they] felt that this was the teacher's responsibility' (Cox et al. 2006: 49). The project highlighted for both adults and children the value of children's own ideas, as Emily, a Year 2 child researcher, commented: 'I think [it is] good if children decide because we have lots of ideas and some are better than adults' (Year 2 Children 2006: 87). Although the risks may have been too great in some cases for teachers to take the children's ideas forward into action, by the end of the project there was some movement towards children making decisions that impacted on significant areas, including their learning and the curriculum.

Conclusion

Awareness of risk became particularly apparent in this action research project where change was an integral part of the process. Our experience in working with children and teachers as researchers revealed that perceptions of risk influenced how far research could lead into change that would make a real difference to classroom lives and cultures. For all concerned – both adults and children – the project served to highlight the tacit assumptions that underpin classroom life and the place of children's research within it. In practice, the research process engaged all the participants in significant learning about the complexities of achieving change in a classroom context. As a Year 4 teacher reflected on the process of action research in her classroom: 'It is not necessarily about making dramatic changes; the changes which developed for our class were more subtle and gradual than this and involved an underlying culture change within the classroom' (Nudd 2006: 150).

Acknowledgements

We would like to acknowledge all the teachers in the 'Children Decide' research team in the nine Norfolk classrooms, who were partners in this research (Daniel Currie, Kath Frederick, De Jarvis, Sue Lawes, Emily Millner, Kirsty Nudd, Isabel Stubbs, Tim Taylor and Debbie White) as well as all the children in their classes. The project would not have been possible without funding from CfBT Education Trust.

References

Cox, S. and Robinson-Pant, A. with B. Elliott, D. Jarvis, S. Lawes, E. Millner and T.Taylor (2003) *Empowering Children through Visual Communication.* CfBT/UEA (available at: www.cfbt.com/research/projects/emp_vis_com.html).

Cox, S., Currie, D., Frederick, K., Jarvis, D., Lawes, S., Millner, E., Nudd, K., Robinson-Pant, A., Stubbs, I., Taylor, T. and White, D. (2006) *Children Decide: Power, Participation and Purpose in the Primary Classroom.* CfBT/UEA Research Report, Norwich (available from Libby.Allen@uea.ac.uk).

Cox, S., Currie, D., Frederick, K., Jarvis, D., Lawes, S., Millner, E., Nudd, K., Robinson-Pant, A., Stubbs, I., Taylor, T. and White, D. (2007) *Children Decide: Power, Participation and Purpose in the Primary Classroom: A Guide for Teachers Based on a Research Project Funded by CfBT Education Trust.* London: CfBT Education Trust.

Currie, D. (2006) ' "RChoice" ' project report', in Cox et al. (2006).

Department for Children, Schools and Families (2008) 'Independent review of the primary curriculum'. http://www.dcsf.gov.uk/primarycurriculumreview/

Jarvis, D. and Frederick, K. (2006) 'Joint project report from Poringland Primary School', in Cox et al. (2006).

Lawes, S. (2006) 'Project report', in Cox et al. (2006).

Millner, E. (2006) 'Project report', in Cox et al. (2006).

Nudd, K. (2006) ' "Sharing decisions" project report', in Cox et al. (2006).

Rudduck, J. (2003) 'Pupil voice and citizenship education', *Report for the QCA Citizenship and PSHE Team, March,* Cambridge University (available at www.qca.org.uk/ages3-14/downloads/Pupil_voice.pdf).

Stubbs, I. (2006) 'Project report', in Cox et al. (2006).

Taylor, T. (2006) ' "Exploring power sharing in the primary classroom" project report', in Cox et al. (2006).

White, D. (2006) ' "Time for a cat stamp" project report', in Cox et al. (2006).

Year 2 children from Mundesley First School (2006) 'The UEA book', in Cox et al. (2006).

Chapter 16

Children's participation: radio as a medium in Ghana

Esmeranda Manful

Introduction

One of the benefits of involving children in decision-making is that they can offer a different perspective and inputs than adults, which might make public issues relevant to them. Although effective participation of children in issues that affect them could occur on different levels and to differing degrees, the important factor is their being given the opportunity. Radio broadcasting is one communication medium which can facilitate children's participation. This chapter discusses an example of child participation in public debate through radio broadcasting in Ghana. It outlines the process of how children participate in live radio broadcasting, by taking charge of the content and hosting of the programme. The benefits and challenges of involving children in such a process are also discussed. It concludes by arguing that children hosting their own radio programme facilitate different levels and degrees of participation, which builds their confidence for active involvement in social issues.

Participation in civil issues occurs in different forms and media, but one important factor is to be able to make opinion public. Children's issues often attract a lot of discussion in the public domain. However, the main stakeholders, children, usually do not participate effectively in such debates. The media have greatly enhanced public participation in civil issues, especially through the growth of an interactive media society alongside the traditional mass media (Carlsson 2006). Yet limited initiatives have been embarked on for children to benefit from the communication medium as a tool to facilitate their participation in public issues. It is acknowledged that the involvement of children and young people in the media is not a recent phenomenon (Feilitzen and Bucht 2001); however, the media as a tool for facilitating the participation process is a recent phenomenon. This chapter argues that children's participation takes different forms, levels and degrees but there must be an opportunity to facilitate the process. It commences by discussing different forms and levels of participation, children and the media and focuses on an example in Ghana, where a process has been adopted to ensure the participation of children in public debate on issues that generally affect their development.

The process of participation

Participation in civil issues occurs on different levels and to differing degrees. Arnstein (1969) argued that there are different levels of participation and non-participation which she depicted in a ladder model. Her ladder has inspired different models of participation for children (Hart 1992; Thoburn et al. 1995; Shier 2001). In these models, instances such as placation, tokenism and manipulation were described as non-participation, whereas situations where children are informed, consulted, listened to and allowed to initiate programmes were described as different levels of participation. These ladders therefore serve as indicators of the level of children's participation in activities.

However, Murray and Hallett (2000) argue that the ladder of participation is derived from an adult conceptualization of citizenship to deal with issues in urban society, and thus has less relevance to children and young people. Nixon (2007) is also of the opinion that the ladders of participation do not recognize the complex interplay of factors that promote or serve as a challenge in the involvement of children. He suggests that children's participation should rather be described in terms of interrelated types of participation, including informing, consulting, partnership and delegating control. One can conclude that the level and degree of participation help in determining an activity as participatory. It also seems the ladders of participation serve as indicators of situations which could be described as participatory or non-participatory. In addition, Nixon's arguments reveal that participation is not a one-off event but involves different types which can be found on different levels and to differing degrees which overlap in some instances. The extent of children's involvement in activities has to be considered in order to declare a process participatory or otherwise.

The importance of child participation in social life has been recognized by adults. Sinclair (2004) argues that children's role in social life has been driven by the recognition of children as consumers of goods and services, their inclusion in the rights agenda by the adoption of the UN Convention on the Rights of the Child, and the new paradigms within social science which involve children in research to understand their perspectives on issues. This might be a reflection of the growing acceptance of children's capabilities of influencing issues that affect them. Hill et al. (2004) argue that children's participation improves policy by making it more sensitive to social needs, and that for children it can be of intrinsic value for their views to be sought. Although children's participation is recognized, the level and degree of their participation is often not made visible. Hill et al. identified that the major barriers to children's participation are adults' perceptions of the risk of losing control of children (see also Chapter 15 of the present volume), and the images of children as vulnerable and irresponsible. An evaluation of the arguments indicates that the participation of children in public life has been recognized as important despite the fact that the independent active role of children in the process has been restricted. The reason for limited children's participation could be attributed to the challenges of how to involve children in public life. One solution is through the media, which could give them the opportunity to participate actively in issues that affect them.

Children and the media

Children and the media seem to generate positive and negative opinions, although it is accepted that the media facilitate their participation in public issues. Gigli (2004) argues that the globalized media bring opportunities to broaden children's outlook and make information more equally accessible, but that they are also a threat to cultural values and identification. She further notes that the advances in technology promise new skills and greater youth participation in society but also increase the risk of child exploitation. Similarly, Livingstone (2002) suggests that optimists share the view that the media in the twenty-first century provide new opportunities for democratic and community participation, whilst pessimists perceive this as the end of childhood, innocence and authority. It appears that these social anxieties can be attributed to the perception of children as vulnerable and in need of protection from the evils of the general society to which the globalized media seem to expose them. The concern is not limited to only one form of communication and its effects on children, but includes every new communication medium which has been invented (Paik 2001). Questions were asked about the introduction of video games before the internet, about the video cassette recorder a couple of decades earlier, about the introduction of television before that, about radio, cinema and comics among others (Livingstone 2002). Nonetheless, the media have changed the process of information exchange in the world which affects both adults and children. The media vary, but all share one goal of making information accessible.

Irrespective of the different forms of communication available to children and young people in the twenty-first century, the radio is still a popular medium. Paik (2001) argues that studies in North America have proved that there exists a heavy usage of radio among children and young people despite the presence of different media forms. Gigli (2004) also notes that after television, listening to radio is the second most popular activity among children and young people world-wide. She comments that in Africa there has been an increase in the numbers of young people listening because of the emergence of private radio stations in recent times. Therefore, it seems that radio could serve dual roles for children and young people; a medium for them to be informed about and through which to participate in public issues. The challenge is how to ensure their effective participation in the development of issues that affect them (Gigli 2004). An example of where children are allowed to participate as initiators with adults' assistance is a radio programme hosted in the state-run Ghana Broadcasting Corporation. It is a programme where children participate in public debate on issues relevant to them and their community.

Children's radio broadcasting in Ghana

The Republic of Ghana is a nation in West Africa. It covers a total area of 239,460 sq. km, very similar that of the United Kingdom (Avoke 2001). Ghana has a young population structure; it is estimated that 48.3 per cent of its total population of 23 million are below 18 years of age (Population Reference Bureau 2007). Half of the population in Ghana live in urban areas and about 97 per cent of children enrol in primary education (United Nations Population Fund 2008). English is the official language and is used in every part of the country as a means of communication beyond the various local Ghanaian languages (Obeng 1997). In the mid-1990s the state controlled all 10 radio stations established in the country; however, deregulation of the airwaves in 1996 led to the introduction of private radio broadcasting (McKay 2003). In 2007 there were estimated to be 89 FM radio stations in the country (CIA 2008). The growth in the number of radio stations is a possible indication that radio is an important communication medium in Ghana.

The club

In 1995, an association of women communicators and journalists organized the International Children's Day of Broadcasting in Ghana. Children who participated in the activities were asked to form a club. The objectives of the formation of the club included the provision of a platform for children and young people to use the electronic media to express their opinions on issues that affect them and to build their confidence in civil issues (Akrofi-Quarcoo 1999).

To be a member of the club one has to be aged 8–17 years. Membership includes children and young people from different ethnic groups who mainly live close to the Ghana Broadcasting Corporation where the club is hosted. A couple of years after its establishment, funding was secured for children to have a 30-minute slot on live radio where they could host their own programmes and discuss issues relevant to the development of children and their rights (Akrofi-Quarcoo 1999). Club meetings are held twice a week, including one meeting day scheduled for the live radio programme. With assistance from adults, the group produces a live magazine which is broadcast once a week. The children and young people work on the development of the programme and serve as producers and anchor. The programme is supervised by a professional journalist who also coordinates the activities of the group.

The format of the radio programme

The 30-minute radio programme has two segments, although the time allotted is at the discretion of the child anchor. It normally commences with a discussion on the topic chosen, then the panel on the live programme share their opinions as to what should be done to ensure the best interest of the child in relation to the topic. The second segment of the programme involves an interaction of the panel with adult experts. It also includes a phone-in segment where children can express their opinion on the topic. This section outlines the activities that lead to the live programme.

Selection of topics

The first meeting day of the week for the club is for topic selection. Members of the club decide on the topic or issue that will be discussed in subsequent weeks. They usually focus on government policies relating to children including education, HIV/AIDS, poverty and street children. The topics are often those that are already in the public domain, on which they express their opinions and perspectives on how their best interest will be ensured. Based on consensus, an issue is chosen for the week. This is discussed and each member is tasked to look for further information.

Choosing participants in the live radio discussion

The decision on who participates is made by the children themselves, without adult interference. The selection of a member to be part of the live programme is based on how well the member is informed and could articulate opinions on the chosen topic. The decision is arrived at after the topic is discussed off-air by the whole group. Usually three members of the club are chosen to be on the panel, where they are joined by a government official or an expert on the topic of discussion. Although few members of the club may be sharing their views on the live programme, the process also gradually builds the confidence of the membership of the club and makes them informed on community issues.

How other children participate in the discussion

The live radio programme enables other children who are not members of the club to participate in issues being discussed through the phone-in facility. Often, this allows children and parents to call into the programme to express an opinion or ask questions. The programme further allows parents, programme developers and policy makers to hear the perspectives of Ghanaian children and young people on issues that are of interest to them.

Achievements

Through the live phone-in radio programme, the club has created a platform where politicians and experts, including the speaker of Ghana's parliament and heads of departments, have interacted directly with children all over the country. For example, children and young people participated in the discussions that led to the first legislation solely on children's issues in Ghana in 1998. Further, children have access to a medium to express their views on issues that affect them, in the same way as adults. It has increased the number of child-related programmes in the media, with an avenue where children can express their views on civil issues. The live radio programme has also been used by politicians and policy makers to test the popularity or otherwise of projects, and ensure that children are sensitized on national policy issues.

Challenges

Using the media as a means to facilitate child participation poses some challenges. Not all children in Ghana have access to a telephone or can afford to call into the live programmes, thus the views of some children are not heard. Secondly, securing funding to continue to air the programme determines how frequently the programme is produced as the radio stations are commercialized and there is no state funding for such programmes. Thirdly, the programme has not been rolled out in all regions of the country. Aside from recognizing geographical limitations, there is also inadequacy of resources. This is a hindrance to radio executives' willingness to replicate similar programmes in other regions of Ghana.

Discussion

The hosting of a live radio programme provides an example of the experiences of the different participatory activities that could benefit children. The process adopted in Ghana as described in this chapter reveals that it is worthwhile to consider the level of participation and also the content of the participatory activities to determine whether such participation is effective or not. Specifically, the establishment of the club was the idea of adults where children were consulted to be members. After a while the degree of participation changed, with children working in partnership with adults. Gradually, it appears, children became more informed and involved in the process of broadcasting and then they were left in charge of programmes, with assistance from adults. The processes adopted are an indication that participation is not static; at different stages children were consulted, informed, had delegated responsibilities and were in charge. The continuing involvement of adults, with their roles changing from initiators to facilitators, is an indication that for children's participation to be effective adults must play a role.

The programme also ensures that the views of children and young people are heard on the radio. Thrusting the views of a hitherto silent significant group into the public domain gradually builds young people's confidence and raises their awareness of civil issues. At the same time, their perspectives are heard in society.

The participatory approaches outlined in this example from Ghana could also be adopted in school or community radio stations to give children and young people the opportunity to participate in public issues that affect them. This will serve as training for children in their future engagement in the democratic processes in their respective societies.

Conclusion

The club in Ghana serves as an example of the processes of children's participation in public issues that affect them. The club has enabled the perspectives of children and young people to be heard by both adults and children. The chapter has revealed that the form of children's participation is not limited to one level or type, but that children can be involved at different stages. The main factor in enhancing children's participation is for them to be given the opportunity.

References

Akrofi-Quarcoo, S. (1999) 'Young broadcasters in Ghana', in C. V. Feilitzen and U. Carlsson (eds), *Children and Media. Image, Education, Participation*. Gothenburg: Nordicom, pp. 337–40.

Arnstein, S. R. (1969) 'A ladder of citizen participation'. *Journal of the American Institute of Planners*, 35(4), 216–24.

Avoke, M. (2001), 'Some historical perspectives in the development of special education in Ghana'. *European Journal of Special Needs Education*, 16, 29–40.

CIA (2008) *CIA World Fact Book*. https://www.cia.gov/library/publications/the-world-factbook/geos/gh.html. Retrieved 20 June 2008.

Carlsson, U. (2006) 'Introduction. Media Governance: Harm and Offence in Media Content', in U. Carlsson (ed.), *Regulation, Awareness, Empowerment: Young People and Harmful Media Content in the Digital Age*. Gothenburg: International Clearinghouse on Children, Youth and Media, pp. 11–19.

Feilitzen, C. von and Bucht, C. (2001) *Outlooks on Children and the Media*. Gothenburg: UNESCO.

Gigli, S. (2004) *Children, Youth and Media around the World: An Overview of Trends & Issues.* New York: UNICEF.

Hart, R. (1992) *Children's Participation: From Tokenism to Citizenship*, Innocenti Essays No. 4. Florence: UNICEF International Child Development Centre.

Hill, M., Davis, J., Prout, A., and Tisdall, K. (2004) 'Moving the participation agenda forward'. *Children and Society*, 18(2), 77–96.

Livingstone, S. (2002) *Young People and New Media*. London: Sage.

McKay, B. (2003) 'Finding and listening to their voices: community radio and adult learning in a Ghanaian fishing village', in *Canadian Association for the Study of Adult Education – Online Proceedings 2003*. http://www.oise.utoronto.ca/CASAE/cnf2003/2003_papers/blythemackayCAS03.pdf. Retrieved 8 July 2008.

Murray, C., and Hallett, C. (2000) 'Young people's participation in decisions affecting their welfare'. *Childhood*, 7(11), 11–23.

Nixon, P. (2007) 'Seen but not heard? Children and young people's participation in family group decision making: Concepts and practice issues'. *American Humane Association*, 22(1), 20–36.

Obeng, S. G. (1997) 'An analysis of the linguistic situation in Ghana'. *African Languages and Cultures*, 10(1), 63–81.

Paik, H. (2001) 'The history of children's use of electronic media', in D. G. Singer and J. L. Singer (eds), *Handbook of Children and the Media*. London: Sage, pp. 7–27.

Population Reference Bureau (2007) *2007 World Population Data Sheet* (Technical Report). Washington: USAID.

Shier, H. (2001) 'Pathways to participation: openings, opportunities and obligations'. *Children and Society*, 15(2), 107–17.

Sinclair, R. (2004) 'Participation in practice: Making it meaningful, effective and sustainable'. *Children and Society*, 18(2), 106–18.

Thoburn, J., Lewis, A., and Shemmings, D. (1995) *Paternalism or Partnership? Family Involvement in the Child Protection Process*. London: HMSO.

United Nations Population Fund (2008) *State of the World Population 2008*. New York: UNFPA.

Chapter 17

Children as research protagonists and partners in governance

P. J. Lolichen

Introduction

Children have been the *objects* of research for centuries. More recently, some researchers have provided the space for children to 'participate' more intimately in the research process; the impact of such research has been more beneficial to children and the resulting policies more constructive. But children all over the world, and especially rights-based children's organizations such as the many working children's unions and movements, have been concerned about the ethics of policy formulation that is informed by research, but does not include them as active *subjects*. This situation contravenes the UN Convention on the Rights of the Child. According to Article 12: 'States Parties shall assure to the child who is capable of forming his or her own views the right to express those views freely in all matters affecting the child, the views of the child being give due weight in accordance with the age and maturity of the child.' Children have a right to investigate their situations and respond to them; they understand their problems better than anyone else; and they are capable of arriving at solutions most suited to them. Article 13 states: 'The child shall have the right to freedom of expression. This right shall include freedom to seek, receive and impart information and ideas of all kinds, regardless of frontiers, either orally, in writing or in print, in the form of art, or through any other media of the child's choice.'

Children's rights have been a highly prioritized agenda of many international and national policy makers, conventions and dialogues, but despite this, the right to participation is the least realized of them all. Children are seldom consulted in decision-making processes and policy formation, and often it is adult service providers who vie with each other to ensure the best interest of the child. Most children have no access to information that is relevant to their lives; the adult world either entirely denies children comprehensive and accurate information, appropriate to their age, ability and need, or makes the process of accessing it both complex and mysterious.

A general disengagement of citizens with political processes and diminished state accountability are often interpreted as a failure of democracy. People's participation is critical to a healthy democracy, but if an individual's socialization – and childhood interactions – do not provide and promote democratic experiences, the 'citizen' does not activate his/her citizenship rights. Children therefore need to learn and experience processes that enable active democratic participation.

Our organization, The Concerned for Working Children (CWC), has been working with children for over 25 years in India. Our objective has been to empower children to enable their participation in governance processes so that they take informed decisions on matters that affect them; our work demonstrates numerous examples of children conducting their own research, documenting processes and using the information collected to advocate for issues of their concern at local, national and international official decision-making forums.

Research by children

Research by children is not about consulting children, or taking their help as information providers/collectors, or using them as key informers or to assist adults in collecting information. Rather, it is a process whereby children themselves identify research needs, set the research framework, design the methodology, develop and administer the tools, consolidate and analyse the findings and use the information to solve their problems. Child researchers generate information and use it as a logical and informed process to bring about change.

Adults and children often approach matters differently. Children are accountable and responsible to the stakeholders, and ensure that the rights of the community are not violated during the research process. They develop their own ethical codes, which they strictly abide by, and share the information they collect with various community stakeholders and arrive at appropriate strategies to deal with the problems by consulting with them. This may contrast with adults' practices, as Box 17.1 illustrates.

Box 17.1 Children's sense of accountability

In 1998, members of Bhima Sangha were working with a data analyst and asked him, 'why are you working as a data analyst?'. He said, 'I've been doing this work over the last 6 years'. 'But why did you start this career?' He said that during his master's degree his college was actively involved in surveying the areas affected by the Lathur earthquake. He had been involved in conducting surveys and analysing data since then. They asked, 'what did you do with the survey data?' 'We gave it to the state government.' 'What did the government do with the data you gave them?' asked the children. 'I don't know; they may have used it to provide houses to the people.' The children persisted, 'did you go back and check, how many people had got houses, or anything else?' He said 'No!' The children shook their heads disapprovingly and narrated to him their survey story. In 1998 Bhima Sangha conducted a socio-economic survey of about 8000 households in Karnataka. During this process, children made strategic interventions, of re-enrolling children in school, applying for ration cards for families, applying for widow and old age pensions, rescuing children engaged in bonded labour, etc. They shared their findings with every stakeholder in the community and authorities; and their survey exercise led to developing action plans for each *gram panchayat*,[1] which have been implemented over the last few years.

Source: Lolichen (2002).

In our experience of facilitating research by children we have found that children can assess their research needs, design the research framework, develop/adapt appropriate methodology, design tools and equip themselves with research skills. They are able to build rapport with communities, publicize their research, identify key information providers and administer their research tools. They can collect, triangulate, consolidate, analyse and update information that is of concern to them – and are thoroughly committed to and honest in the entire process of research. As one such researcher reported: 'We missed our playtime, free time and even marriage celebrations! But, we are very proud that we were able to do something for our village. We have identified our problems, we know the solutions and also how to get them solved.' If the process is facilitated well, children ensure that the information is complete and correct – and are often better researchers than 'professional researchers'.

At the first children's *grama sabha* in India in 2004, Vinay Kumar Sorake MP said:

Children have pointed out very specific problems and have also suggested specific solutions. All their points have been backed with detailed statistics. Most of the adult Panchayats or the concerned departments do not have such in depth information. I highly appreciate the fact that children first conducted surveys and held discussions among themselves before present-ing the points here.

Children doing their own research

CWC has facilitated working children and underprivileged school children aged 6–18 to design and conduct their own research on issues that they have identified. Their subsequent ability to use this information with the local governments to negotiate solutions and the non-confrontational way of dealing with adults in positions of power, converting these dealings into 'win–win' situations, has been astounding. They showed that they are capable of objectivity, willing to look at multiple sources of information, and have the urgency to act on the information gathered and eagerness to share it with their peers and community (Box 17.2).

Box 17.2 Children validating data

During a study conducted by Bhima Sangha in 1998 (Lolichen 2002), the child researchers reviewed and distinguished between reliable and unreliable data. They classified information they collected as follows:

Accurate
Slightly doubtful
Very doubtful

Housing condition
Income of the family
Chronic diseases

Primary and secondary occupation
Age of teenage girl children
Assets owned by the rich

Assets owned by poor
Amount of land owned
Loans taken by families

Land owned by poor households
Expenditure pattern
Expenditure on alcohol

They made this analysis based on their observation and understanding, especially since they were from the same locality. They consulted multiple sources, including the local revenue office, the government fair price shop, land registration office, local alcohol shop, bank, etc., but were not absolutely sure of some information.

Source: Lolichen (2002)

Children are no less intelligent than adults, but are less informed and experienced. They are capable of abstraction, verification, rigourous work, objectivity and logical thinking. However, for children to successfully engage in research, the process and 'rules' need to be explained clearly and the process made engaging and simple. Children are capable of understanding complexities; so one needs to be careful not to water down the rigour of the process or make the process simplistic, but just simplified. In dealing with children of different ages and ability, the methods used need to be adapted to their needs, enabling all children to participate. For example, the questionnaires and data collection sheets that the children developed during a recent study on their transport and mobility problems were designed to have graphic representations of the questions allowing illiterate children or even the very young to participate.

Children have also shown us their ability to create their own very innovative tools and methods for data collection (Box 17.3).

Box 17.3 Children's data collection tools

Mapping tool – flash cards: five different sets of illustrated cards, each set representing different indicators, such as the individual respondent, different resources the respondent accesses, mode of transport respondent uses, obstacles/hindrances in accessing the resource and seasons cards. Using these cards the respondent discussed and documented various mobility and access problems that he/she faced and possible solutions.

Plotting tool (paper scroll) and observation mapping tool (a long scrollable sheet of paper). Children developed a list of indicators to be observed as they walked along a particular route which they frequented, and assigned symbols for the indicators (such as footbridge, potholes, narrow path, thickly forested areas, lonely areas, shady trees, open wells, gradients, and streams). As they walked they sketched the road and mapped any indicators from their checklist that appeared.

Frequency tool (traffic counts). Child researchers dressed as traffic inspectors, stood at junctions that children frequent, with weighing scales and data sheets, to take a count and collect details of children who carry loads. In this case too they used an illustrated checklist to collect information.

Source: CWC (2006)

For child researchers the process of research is as empowering as the outcome of the research itself, if not more so. Children from Ghana who conducted research on their transport and mobility problems recount this (Box 17.4).

Box 17.4 Perspectives of children from Ghana, trained by CWC

During the workshop, we learned the importance of us having information about our problems. We also learned about various methods of research and designing tools to do the research. Subsequently we conducted the research in the villages that surround our school. Most of us come from these villages. Some of us board. We collected information from school going and working children. The findings from the study were many, some of which surprised us as well. We discussed the findings of the study with our cabinet minister for transport, and other stakeholders during a seminar, trying to find solutions to the issues that we identified. We have already solved some of the smaller problems, which we ourselves could solve.

After we returned to our school from the workshop and the research, we discussed our research and all that we learned with our friends. This led to the forming of a child rights club. We have named our club 'Children's Rights Research Club'. We have over 30 members as of now. Our aim is to identify children's problems and find ways of solving them. We have developed certain rules and regulations for the club and criteria for membership. We meet together at least once a week.

We identified that some children in our boarding school did not eat in the dining hall and a lot of food was wasted. So we trained our other club members in some of the research methods that we learned and prepared appropriate tools for conducting focus group discussions and interviews. We also observed a group of children at the dining hall for a week. We conducted the study and presented the findings to the school management. Our study showed that older girls, who had boy friends, took them out to eat; some richer children who had pocket money would buy snacks from outside. Since many of the richer children were not keen about eating dinner, the authorities were not maintaining the quality of food provided. So poorer children suffered. When this was brought to the notice of the school authorities, necessary actions were taken to rectify the problem.

We want these clubs to grow both within the school and outside to the neighbouring villages.

Kate, Ibrahim, Patience & Sebastian Breman Asikuma Secondary School, Asikuma, Mankesim, Ghana, 2005

Source: CWC (2006)

Children as informed protagonists

Children are the best advocates for their own rights, for they know their situation best: their advocacy strategies are not based on party or class; they are not manipulative, exploitative or discriminatory. Research and resulting advocacy by children has successfully enabled the active participation of children in democratic processes as informed citizens. Children we work with have been able to influence decisions at various levels, from the lowest social unit to the highest national/international arenas of governance (CWC 2004).

Over the past few years, to strengthen the process of decentralization, the government of India has been attempting to invigorate civil society participation in decision-making processes for policy and governance. But with little state effort and commitment, this vision has not been realized. The state of Karnataka demonstrated some interest, but took no concrete steps until, in 2004, a revolution took place. For the first time, children not only participated, but also led the way for adults to participate, in the 10th National Five-Year planning process, in all 56 *gram panchayats* of Kundapur Taluk, Udupi district, Karnataka. Children in each village and ward gathered together, consulted and discussed, backing their case with statistical information, prepared their five-year plan and presented it to the *gram panchayat*. This has been incorporated into the 10th National Five-Year Plan and is being implemented on a priority basis. This entire process was monumental because it not only rejuvenated people's eagerness to become involved in democratic processes; it was made possible through children's initiatives. Children turned the traditional 'top-down' power structure on its head and demonstrated that they are fully capable of actively participating in decision-making and civil society processes.

Children find that information is a powerful tool and argue with facts and figures, so they offer convincing arguments, rather than emotional pleading. Information management by children enables them to share information among their own peer groups, to interact effectively and to negotiate situations powerfully; it helps them to contribute significantly to consultations as well as advocate for their rights with various stakeholders. This entire process empowers them to take informed decisions, participate in governance, and thus take charge of their lives. Children's participation in governance is not an end in itself, but a process that empowers them to become advocates for social change and transformation.

Adults as facilitators

Adults have a strategic role to play in the process of children doing their own research, as facilitators, enabling the research by playing a balanced role in supporting the processes initiated by children to bring them to a logical conclusion. Children should be facilitated to design their own research, based on their needs. Adults should not impose research agendas on them, nor should they manipulate or take over research initiated by children; but they must deconstruct research in such a way that children are able to grasp the scientific and complex aspects of research in a simple (but not simplistic) and child-friendly manner. Children should be introduced and oriented to various research methodologies so that they can adapt any and put them to use, with adult support. Adults should deconstruct the complex myth of research into processes that are understandable and doable by children, helping them translate their 'desire' to use information as a tool for negotiation into a 'process' of rigour and validity from which they learn to draw their own conclusions – which may be very different from those adults might draw.

A critical role for adults is creating for children an enabling environment where children have trust and confidence, both among themselves and in the process that they set in motion, and can question everything and tear apart existing notions in order to re-examine them. Such an enabling environment should be democratic and transparent, where children feel and experience equality and mutual trust, and free of any discrimination and bias. While the whole process of research should be serious and responsible, it should also enjoyable for the young researchers: '[This was] the first instance where there was child participation in planning and decision-making. There was no gender inequality, no caste discrimination, and children were given a lot of respect. We were very happy in this environment' (A child research protagonist, quoted in CWC 2006).

Children will ensure that their information is shared among all the concerned parties. One of the most important roles adults can play here is to facilitate an effective interface with appropriate decision makers and decision-making structures, so that children can advocate with them to solve their problems. Adults also have a critical role of ensuring children's protection, both physical and emotional. Children should not be exposed to harmful situations; adults should pre-empt and make such environments friendly and adaptable for children.

Conclusion

Children's participation in research and social planning is not an end in itself, but rather a process that continuously needs to be re-evaluated, altered and evolved according to their needs. Research and advocacy by children have successfully enabled their active participation in democratic processes. They are leading the way in making governments accountable. Children have started a revolution for change and the adult world has yet to catch up with them and respond adequately.

Notes

[1] A *panchayat* is composed of a cluster of villages. *Gram panchayat* refers to the geographical and administrative units, as well as the elected body, which is the local government.

References

The Concerned for Working Children (2004) *A Unique Revolution: Children Lead the Way to Decentralisation and Civil Society Participation*. Bangalore: CWC.

The Concerned for Working Children (2006) *Taking a Right Turn: Children Lead the Way in Research*. Bangalore: CWC.

Lolichen P. J. (2002) *Children and Their Own Research: A Process Document*. Bangalore: CWC.

Endpiece: What can we learn about children as decision makers by bringing together perspectives and experiences from different cultures?

Sue Cox, Caroline Dyer, Anna Robinson-Pant and
Michele Schweisfurth

One of the stimuli behind bringing together this volume was the diversity of meanings that individual authors gave to children's participation in decision-making. From the accounts included in this collection, we can see many issues that are shared around the world, and others which derive from questions that are very often specific to a particular context. This concluding piece identifies and explores key questions and themes which individual chapters have addressed from their different cultural perspectives.

What are the purposes and perceptions of participation in different cultural contexts?

This question underlies all the chapters in this volume, and contributors vary in how far they see participation in decision-making as the primary aim of the projects or approaches they describe. Dhankar (Chapter 12) notes that where teachers consciously aim to develop a more democratic approach to learning in the classroom, the deeply entrenched inequalities that pervade wider society can be mitigated and even challenged. Carnie (Chapter 9) and Chiwela (Chapter 6) in turn discuss structures that intentionally aim to enhance children's participation in decision-making in the UK and Zambia, respectively. But pupil participation can also lack democratic intent, or become distorted if, as McCowan (Chapter 2) reminds us, it is valued in the context of a politically driven accountability agenda for its instrumental role in promoting school effectiveness and improvement, increases in test scores, and improvements in the behaviour of pupils.

Authors reflecting on developing country contexts often also reveal further dimensions of complexity associated with cross-cultural borrowing, particularly in relation to models of participation and schooling. The dominant authoritarian model of mass schooling introduced by colonialism is discussed by Harber (Chapter 4), for example. Bhattarai's (Chapter 5) topic of children's clubs in Nepal raises another, more recent influence – that of international non-governmental organizations importing a particular viewpoint on approaches to children's participation. These influences need to be seen in relation to pre-existing and parallel practices indigenous to particular communities, which also shape understandings of participation, including the relationships between children and adults, and schooling and the community.

Another prominent theme is the contribution which children's participation in decision-making might make in strengthening democratic structures in society at large. As democracy in many contexts appears to disappoint, and fails to excite popular participation, authors argue for the need for children to experience democratic processes and to be able to contribute to social change. In the UK context, the projects described here focused on the school as the context for children's decision-making. Yet schools are a bounded space and, as some contributors here point out, institutional norms can promote but also restrict children's participation; and they may also specify arenas where it is encouraged as 'appropriate' and where it is not. For example, it may be promoted as appropriate in a school council discussion about lunches, but not in a meeting about curriculum. Various contributors explore tensions of extrinsic and intrinsic motivations for participation in decision-making. Yamashita et al. (Chapter 10) reflect on this question as it arises from their literature review – is children's participation primarily motivated by an underlying belief that this will result in better decisions, or because it results in a personal benefit that is of itself valuable?

The differences in emphasis cannot be explained simply in terms of a divide between developed and developing countries. They remind us to challenge possible assumptions about the nature and origins of the participation agenda – see Cooke and Kothari (2001) on the 'tyranny of participation' – and to reflect on the influence of local cultural practices and structures. 'Participation' is a dynamic, complex and contested notion. It is, as Aikman (Chapter 3) reminds us, intrinsically linked to questions of both agency, and visible, hidden and invisible power.

How do notions of childhood impact on children's roles in decision-making?

All the authors, either implicitly or explicitly, question what childhood means in the communities they describe, and in so doing underline the need to recognize the plurality of childhoods. This emerges through these chapters in, for example, the distinction made between being a child and being an adult, the relationships between children and adults, their levels of autonomy and differing responsibilities. The idea that childhood is a stage of life associated with chronological age (reflected, for example, in the definition of childhood (0–18) in the UN Convention on the Rights of the Child) is an individualistic interpretation: it limits personal responsibility within a context of parental or community belonging. But it may not resonate in contexts where a child of school-going age may already carry the full responsibilities of being the head of a household, or be the main income earner for their whole family.

Many of these chapters illustrate the range of roles and expectations of children and how these are culturally situated. Childhood can also be understood as constructed by discourses, a fluid concept that can, in any one context, be shaped by influences from different cultures. This is well captured from the Nepali context by Bhattarai's demonstration of how these questions can be explored both in terms of traditional Hindu religious beliefs and practices as well as imported educational ideas from Britain, which prescribed how adults should treat children.

Alongside these beliefs which assume that adults have power over children, there may be expectations about the role that children should play in contributing to family livelihood. While this could be seen as giving children adult-like responsibility for earning an income, there are still questions around how far children have status and autonomy. A significant question underlying several authors' contributions is the extent to which adults regard children's decision-making as preparation for adult life, or as having meaning in its own right. Richards, writing from a UK perspective, asks in Chapter 1: 'are we simply (but importantly) helping them to understand their future roles as citizens or are we helping them to develop here and now as participatory school citizens?' Trippett et al. (Chapter 7) note the relative freedom experienced by children in developing country contexts where, for example, their participation in decision-making is less constrained by practices such as health and safety risk assessments.

In those cultural contexts where the boundaries between adult and child responsibilities are more blurred, there may be more opportunity for children to take their part in real life decision-making. In contexts where educational participation is not universal, horizons extend into structures of governance and encompass the wider community. Then, the children's 'world' is conceptualized not merely in terms of school and home, as often reflected in examples from developed country contexts; rather, their decisions have enduring impacts on not only their own, but also adults' lives. Lolichen's starting point in Chapter 17, for example, is the child as a potential decision maker in community governance (the *panchayat*) and as a research protagonist. Manful (Chapter 16) describes children's contribution in the public domain of radio broadcasting. Unusually in the UK contributions, Smith (Chapter 8) describes how children working on the fairtrade project within their schools welcomed the opportunity to influence adults' behaviour in the wider community.

In what ways does 'school' constrain children's decision-making?

Across the range of cultural contexts, mass public schooling is conceived as a particularly problematic arena for children's decision-making. Describing schools as 'places of unfreedoms', quoting from Nelson Mandela Foundation (2005), Harber talks about the dominance of 'education for control' in the real world of schooling, as compared with education 'for critical consciousness'. Many of the authors address issues around constraints that arise specifically because they are discussing children's decision-making within the domain of the formal school. Fowler (Chapter 14), for instance, considers the challenges of creating more collegiate relationships between teachers and students; Cox and Robinson-Pant (Chapter 15) discuss the ways in which teachers and children negotiate 'risks' that are encountered when children take on action research within their classrooms; and Springate and Lindridge (Chapter 13) address the limits to children's power that can be addressed through children undertaking research.

Many of these authors are addressing issues of power and the contours of adult–children relationships, particularly in schooling contexts. They also raise important questions about whether children's decision-making is something that adults genuinely embrace, or experience as imposed upon them and a threat to their authority. At worst, this can lead to a 'box ticking' approach that allows children to make decisions only on what Smith characterizes as 'tame areas'. However, many accounts of attempts to challenge school cultures show evidence that transformation can be achieved – and in very different ways. New approaches can effectively disrupt old routines both within a single school and, as Carnie shows, on a city-wide scale. Dhankar shows at the micro level how reflexive teachers can create a classroom culture of equal opportunity to participate – but he is mindful of the enormous challenges of transferring this culture to a large public system of education. Sometimes change has a more dramatic starting point. Aikman, for example, reports on the unique opportunity for transformation that resulted from conflict in Mindanao, when normal structures and educational practices were disrupted. Barrón-Pastor (Chapter 11) reflects on the opportunity provided – but also missed – by a public policy shift in Mexico, and his account cautions against a superficial policy understanding of what needs to change. In this case, participation was not able to advance sufficiently to interrupt undemocratic relations of power and dominance that continue to disadvantage those whose cultural norms are interpreted as inferior.

Understanding sustainability and change

The impact of children's participation in decision-making remains difficult to quantify and evaluate. In part this is, as we have discussed above, because participation itself is such a diffuse and slippery concept, serving simultaneously as both a means and an end, and shaped very differently by the contexts in which is it exercised. Importantly, however, it is also difficult to 'measure' in both the short and longer term. As Yamashita et al. argue, participation simply cannot be isolated as a variable with a particular causal effect – and where attempts are made to do this, correlations are all too readily confused with causality. It is also a – perhaps frustrating – characteristic of educational change that the full impact of actions carried out today is often not visible until several years later. Another challenge in understanding impact is that much of the work reported on here is project based, bringing with it constraints of a short time frame and questions over longer-term sustainability – of both changes made, and resources to support future effort. These questions are clearly addressed by Tippett et al., for example, who point out the desirability of embedding individual projects within larger, long-term sectoral effort to realize the aims of the Convention on the Rights of the Child.

However, a view emerges from these accounts that where children's participation in decision-making is able to speak to power, it has demonstrable impact. The chapters reporting on interactions with community and governance (Chiwela, Lolichen, and Tripett et al.) offer optimism that children's greater visibility in processes of change has brought new respect from adults, and kindled new understandings of children's vast potential as development actors. Where the focus is more closely within schools, there remains a nagging doubt about how pupil voice will ride the ever-changing winds of educational policy.

References

Cooke, B. and Kothari, U. (2001) *Participation: The New Tyranny?* London: Zed Books.
Nelson Mandela Foundation (2005) *Emerging Voices*. Cape Town: HSRC Press.

Index